A Fancier's Guide

LOP RABBIT

by

GEOFF RUSSELL

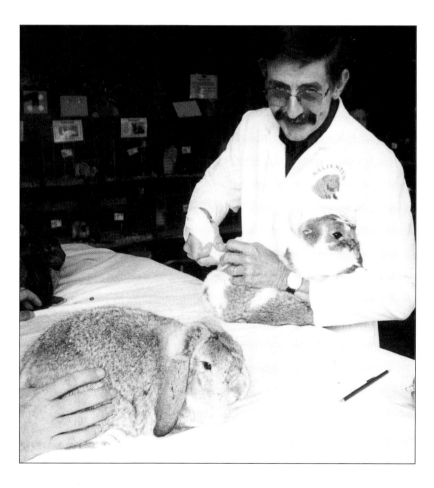

Copyright 2004 by
Coney Publications
Chattisham, Ipswich, Suffolk IP8 3QE

Other titles in this series:
The Beginner's Guide to the Cashmere Lop
    by Jean Wolstenholme.
The Beginner's Guide to the English Angora
    by Barbara Pratley and Yvonne Hobbs
A Fancier's Guide to the Netherland Dwarf
    by Phil Birch.
A Fancier's Guide to the Rex Rabbit
    by John Hodgkiss
Rabbit Nutrition
    by Virginia Richardson.

ISBN 1-898015-06-6

Set in 11 Baskerville,
printed and bound in Great Britain
by K.D.S.,
Ipswich, Suffolk.

Foreword

It is now some fifty years since I had the privilege of judging some of the first French Lops to be exhibited in Britain. Since then I have watched with interest the rise in the popularity of the lops, to the point where we now have eight breeds that have their own diploma and compete on equal terms for Best in Show with all the other breeds.

I have known Geoff since he first started showing rabbits and have judged his lops for many years. A dedicated exhibitor, Geoff rarely misses a weekend show even if he has to travel many miles to find one. The outcome of Geoff's dedication to his breeding and showing programmes is that he now frequently figures in the results and his example to all is that champion lops can be bred if you persevere, read everything on rabbits that you can, attend as many shows as you can and learn as much as you can.

Geoff's easy style of writing means that his monthly column in *Fur and Feather* is extremely popular as are his numerous other articles on rabbits, rabbit husbandry and showing. It therefore gives me great pleasure to endorse this book on Lops. I am sure it will give many people many happy hours of reading.

Bernard Trute

Introduction

During the last twenty years or so Lop Rabbits have returned to the popularity they enjoyed a hundred years ago but in a very different way. If I had been writing a book on Lop Rabbits a hundred years ago it would have been entitled 'The Lop Rabbit', for there was only one breed of lop rabbit being exhibited in Britain and it was simply known as 'The Lop'. We now call that lop the 'English Lop' and have seven other breeds of lop rabbit whose Breed Standard has been accepted by the British Rabbit Council. Lops in all their various guises now account for over 25% of the total entry of all rabbits at the annual Bradford Championship Show.

Although it would be virtually impossible to make an accurate estimate of the number of Lop Rabbits that are currently being kept as pets in Britain I know from personal experience, having owned a pet shop for ten years, that the demand for lops as pets is insatiable. The rabbit is now the third most popular pet in Britain and it is probably a conservative estimate to say that half of all those pet rabbits are lops. Of course many of these pet lops do not meet the requirements of the B.R.C breed standards but that does not matter in the least; they are adorable, appealing, friendly rabbits that make ideal house rabbits and outdoor pets.

In writing this book I have tried to cover the needs of both the pet and show lop keeper and breeder. Hopefully there is something in the book for all lop keepers. I have deliberately omitted a chapter on ailments and diseases as there are numerous excellent books that cover this aspect far better than I, but I have included a detailed chapter on colour for two reasons:

Firstly because I believe that it is an area of lop breeding that still . requires a considerable amount of work by those who dedicate themselves to the pursuit of excellence. Secondly, because there is currently no book available that brings together in one chapter all the colours and their requirements.

I am the first to admit that I do not know everything there is to know about lops and am deeply grateful to all the wonderful friends I have in the Rabbit Fancy who have supplied me with detailed information and the background knowledge that has enabled me to write what I hope will become a useful and informative guide to all those who love and own lops.

Geoff Russell
2004

Acknowledgements

It is to the numerous un-named Fanciers of the British Rabbit Council who I encounter and listen to at every show I attend that I must give my greatest thanks, for it is their knowledge that has unwittingly contributed to my personal background knowledge allowing me the honour of writing this book.

I am most grateful to Deb Goodenough for her speedy and accurate editing of all the material in this book and to the breed specialists namely Pat and Jane Duffy (Miniature Lop), Hazel and Sarah Elliott (French and Dwarf Lop), Deb Goodenough and Phil Wheeler (English Lop), Avril and Leighton Davies (German Lop), Simon Whincup (Cashmere and Mini Cashmere Lop), Owen and Lindsay Davies (Meissner Lop) and Judy LeMarchant who have all freely given their time to read and comment on my drafts.

I would also like to record my sincere thanks to Pat Gaskin for having faith in me and allowing me to write this book for Coney Press, and to all the unsung, backroom staff at *Fur and Feather* and Coney Press for their hard work and dedication without which there would be no book.

Finally I would like to thank my wife, Lynn for her patience and encouragement.

Contents

Foreword 3

Acknowledgements 5

Chapter One: Why Lops 7

Chapter Two: Buying Lops 12

Chapter Three: Housing Lops 20

Chapter Four: Maintaining Lops 34

Chapter Five: Breeding Lops 51

Chapter Six: Showing Lops 70

Chapter Seven: The Cashmere Lop 94

Chapter Eight: The Dwarf Lop 104

Chapter Nine: The English Lop 114

Chapter Ten: The French Lop 126

Chapter Eleven: The German Lop 136

Chapter Twelve: The Meissner Lop 145

Chapter Thirteen: The Miniature Lop 152

Chapter Fourteen: The Miniature Cashmere Lop 164

Chapter Fifteen: The Colours of the Lop 168

Chapter Sixteen: The Future of the Lop 199

Glossary of Common Terms 202

Further Recommended Reading 214

Photographs:
The author would like to thank Lea Fletcher and all Lop fanciers who contributed or who gave permission for their rabbits to be photographed.
Other photographs from *Fur & Feather* archives and by the author.

Chapter 1
Why Lops

Best pals: Mitchell Pooley and his pet Lop Harry

W HY HAVE LOPS become so popular; why are so many people now showing lops, why are so many pets and especially house rabbits lops?

Until the events of the early 1950's it was the norm to either keep rabbits for their meat or their fur. This meant that big fast growing rabbits with thick lustrous coats were the most popular; this invariably meant the New Zealand White.

The English Lop, considered by many as the 'King of the Fancy', was the most popular Fancy (i.e. show) rabbit during the latter part of the nineteenth century and early part of the twentieth century. Its popularity declined throughout the twentieth century because it was considered unsuitable as a meat or fur rabbit and with two World Wars and the Great Depression food production was of paramount importance.

During the first half of the twentieth century rabbits were kept in any available space, in the backyard of even the smallest of terraced houses or quite often on an allotment when there was no back yard. They were mainly kept for their meat to provide the family with high quality protein.

During the second world war people were encouraged to keep rabbits for meat and were allocated a bran ration to feed the rabbits with. Most were fed on a combination of wild herbage and had the bran, boiled with, among other things, potato peelings in a 'mash'.

Even though the Fancy thrived throughout this period and shows often had far higher entries than now, most show rabbits were those that could be eaten, or had a pelt that could be sold to furriers.

In the years following the Second World War much social change took place in Britain and it was to have a great effect on the nation's rabbit keeping habits. The end of bran rationing in itself probably did not have a great effect and in fact was probably one of the reasons why many rabbit keepers developed a variety of mash recipes utilising all manner of household scraps.

The post war baby boom did, however, bring about social changes to our way of life that were to revolutionise rabbit keeping in Britain. New Towns were built across the country to accommodate the overspill from major cities; rather than convert the city dwellers to a country lifestyle it had the effect of urbanising once rural areas.

The aspirations of the population changed. No longer was the garden the place to provide food for the table; the family food started to come from the supermarkets. Ordinary working people owned cars and televisions and leisure time was to be irreversibly changed.

Whilst the working day has almost certainly got shorter for the majority of people, many now commute arriving home late into the evening. An average household has all members working so that no one is at home throughout the day.

Although the keeping of rabbits for meat declined throughout the fifties and sixties, it was, throughout this period, quite the norm to see wild rabbits hanging outside a butchers shop.

In 1953 Myxomatosis arrived in Britain from France, first being identified at Edenbridge, Kent in June of that year. The disease rapidly spread throughout the country, albeit often deliberately by farmers trying to reduce the damage rabbits caused to their crops.

The disease killed 90% of the wild rabbit population and was to gradually reduce the sales of wild rabbit through retailers, so that by the mid to late sixties it was very unusual to find rabbit for sale. But myxomatosis also had a devastating effect on the keepers of exhibition and pet rabbits. Many breeders lost entire studs, and an unknown number of pet rabbits died the horrible death that myxomatosis causes if untreated.

One outcome of all this social change was that rabbits were no longer part of the family's food chain and were kept either as fancy (show) rabbits, or as pets. This was to have an enormous effect on the membership of the British Rabbit Council (BRC) and their rabbit keeping habits. Because exhibition rabbits were bred in an attempt to achieve the perfection of the standard, then there was no longer any need to keep large rabbits.

Many women came into the Fancy, often using it as an interesting hobby to share with their children. The combined effect of these social changes was a general move towards smaller rabbits. It was this opening that was to bring about the rise in popularity of the lops.

Why is it that lops have benefited from all this change when there are many other small breeds? It must really come down to the cuteness of the young lop. Bearing in mind what has been written previously about the vast increase in women/children keeping and showing rabbits, it is no surprise that the cuteness of the young lop, combined with its small size (certainly of the most popular lop – the Miniature

Lop) is responsible for its increase in popularity.

Bearing in mind that most pet purchasers want to buy their baby rabbit when it is as young and small as possible, it is no wonder that the six week old miniature lop, sold by what can only be described as unscrupulous dealers, is so popular.

During the late twentieth century the House Rabbit became popular. Its perceived needs fitted the lifestyle of many working families – sleeps most of the day, easy to feed and keep clean, comes out for a play in the evening and early morning, is quiet and can quite easily be house trained. This was again to favour the lop, but often the bigger lop. The French Lop seemed ideally suited to the house rabbits' life style, being big and cuddly with a very laid back demeanour so suiting the working family who could give and receive the rabbit's attention when not at work.

It would appear that lops, ranging in size from the Miniature at about 3lb to the French averaging about 14lbs, have found their way into the hearts of both the exhibitor and the pet owning public. Whilst no figures are available for the number of lops in pet

Lops on the judging table at Bradford Championship Show

ownership we can see the increase in lops being exhibited at our shows over the years.

As recently as 1986 a total of only 123 lops were shown at the UK's largest rabbit show, the Bradford Championship Show. In 2003, 294 lops were exhibited.

Another indicator of the lops' rise in popularity as a show rabbit is that, following pressure from exhibitors, around 2000 the British Rabbit Council was forced to introduce the Lop Diploma and thus give the Lop a Section of its own. As a Section winner the best lop would automatically go forward to be judged on equal terms with the other Section winners for Best in Show.

An article was published in the 2003 National Miniature Lop Rabbit Club 'Year Book' that showed a distinct change in the ownership of Miniature Lops over the first six years of the club's existence. In 1996 when the Club was formed the membership distribution showed clear pockets around the built up areas of the country. However, by 2002 the distribution was evenly spread throughout most of the country.

Whilst the British Rabbit Council membership figures have declined throughout this period the percentage of members showing lops has dramatically increased.

Again, this is a difficult statement to prove without looking at the Bradford Ch Show figures. In 1986 the proportion of lops to all rabbits shown at Bradford was 8.43%. This percentage rose to 17.6% in 2003.

Surely it will not be too long before a fifth of all entries will be lops. A significant rise, and one that proves that the ownership and exhibiting of lops is certainly on the increase.

Will it continue to rise, will it level out or will it tail off? Of course these are questions that only history or a clairvoyant can answer, but we can assume that other new breeds will be introduced in the future and also become popular; in doing so this will probably reduce the numbers of new exhibitors coming into the various lop breeds.

However, with eight breeds ranging in size from very small to very large, a wonderful disposition and ever improving quality of stock it is hard to foresee a decline in lop ownership in the immediate future.

Chapter 2
Buying Lops

W E HAVE ALL HEARD THE SLOGAN "A Dog is for Life not just for Christmas". This applies equally to rabbits, who are a 365 day a year commitment.

Rabbits must be fed and watered every day and as social animals they need regular companionship. They must be kept in a secure environment, secure from outside dangers and secure to prevent them escaping.

You must ask yourself 'is your life style ready to accept another member of the family that can be given the time and affection it deserves?'

When buying a lop rabbit you must make some big decisions before you even approach a breeder.

First, you must decide the breed that will best suit your aspirations.

There is a vast difference between a Miniature Lop that will only weigh about 3lb 8ozs at adulthood, and a French Lop that may well have an adult weight of about 15lbs.

If you want to show your lop then you must visit some shows and look at all the different breeds so that you know what the alternatives are. It is there that you can talk to exhibitors and you will find that the vast majority of breeders will only be too happy to speak to you about their breed.

What sex of rabbit do you want? If you intend to keep your lop as a pet then you must consider the physical and temperamental differences.

Generally speaking bucks make better pets as they are usually more playful and have more character. The downside of a pet buck is that some become 'sprayers' when they mature sexually and this can be quite unpleasant, especially if it is a child's pet. However, having the buck castrated can usually stop him 'spraying'.

Whilst many does grow into affectionate adults there will be periods when she will become quite grumpy and start nest building, it is not uncommon at this time for them to bite the hand that feeds them. It is in every doe's nature to produce young and if you do not intend breeding from them then it is perhaps best that you buy a buck rather than a doe.

If you intend to show your lop then you should be aware that generally speaking only buck lops are shown as adults. Either bucks or does may be shown as under five month young stock.

With the exception of Cashmere and Mini Cashmere Lops, does are generally not shown as adults because you will see in the breed standards that a broad skull is required and again, generalising, does do not have the width of skull characteristic of bucks. Also, the breed standards state that a dewlap is undesirable. Only does have dewlaps, so do not show adult does (except Cashmere and Mini Cashmere lops that do not seem to suffer from lack of skull width or excessive dewlaps).

If you are going to show your lop then it must be properly prepared for each show (see Chapter 6 Showing Lops). This will mean turning it upside down to groom the underneath and clean the feet, a task that is considerably easier on the Miniature Lop than it is for an English or French Lop.

Large rabbits need large hutches (see Chapter 3 Housing Lops), they require a lot of bedding and generate a lot of waste that must be disposed of. You must have a regular supply of food, (not such a problem these days now when even Supermarkets that are open seven days a week sell rabbit food).

Whether you want your lop as a pet or for showing and breeding purposes, you want a healthy specimen that is not carrying a latent disease or visible or genetic problems. The only way to do this is to buy from a reputable breeder.

The breeder must keep his stock in sanitary conditions and any breeder who values his stock will take pride in his rabbitry. A filthy, untidy rabbitry indicates poor stockmanship and should be avoided. Similarly, anyone selling rabbits cheaply who cannot sex or handle them should be avoided.

The genuine breeders who take pride in their animals will easily be spotted, they will talk freely and knowledgably, they will handle their stock in a kind manner that respects the animal.

But there is a lot more to look for. Because lops are naturally so appealing it is easy to be taken in by their cuteness when they are young. Buying rabbits from anyone who is less than reputable is only perpetuating their trade and buying in trouble for yourself in the future. The guidelines that follow are intended to make sure that you buy a healthy animal with a pleasant demeanour who will not only give you years of happiness but also lead a happy and healthy life.

1. Only buy through a reputable breeder. You can find the breeders in your area by contacting the British Rabbit Council, or by visiting one of your local shows. However, the fact that the would-be sellers are at a show or are a member of the BRC is not in itself a guarantee that they are reputable.

2. Visit the rabbitry. This is most important as it is only in the rabbitry that you will see how the rabbits are kept.

The rabbitry should be well managed and clean, with rabbits kept singly in large spacious cages. Rabbits are inquisitive and they should come to the front of the cage when you approach it, not cower in the corner at the back.

3. There should be a quarantine section somewhere separate from

the main rabbitry. No matter how good a rabbitry is, there should be somewhere to isolate a new rabbit coming in or one showing any signs of illness. If there is no such isolation area then you must assume that all rabbits are kept together whether healthy or not and this is not a sign of good management.

4. Does the breeder advertise his stud bucks for use to other breeders? If so then you should clearly see these stud animals kept permanently isolated from the rest of the stock.

5. You should ask to see and if possible handle the parents of the rabbit you are intending to buy. If they are not of a pleasant disposition then ask yourself what your little bundle of fluff might grow up to be like.

6. Mentally prepare yourself a checklist. This is similar to what every judge does with every rabbit he picks up on the show bench.

You may think, watching a judge, that he couldn't possibly check all these points in such a short space of time. But he does, albeit very quickly and with experience, very skilfully.

If you feel confident enough to carry out the physical checks yourself, ask the owner if he minds you handling the rabbit and checking it over. If you do not feel confident enough to carry out these checks, you could ask the owner to show you each of the following points. If these checks are not carried out with both you and the owner present then you can only rely on the owner's honesty and will not have any recourse should something turn out to be other than you had been lead to expect.

So either yourself, or the owner with you watching, check the following:

Start at the front of the rabbit and work towards the back end checking all of the following:

Nose – should be clear and dry with no discharge.

Teeth – should be clean and white. The top teeth should just overlap the bottom ones. Do not be fobbed off if the teeth meet and the breeder tells you that they will come right as they grow older – they won't.

Eyes - should be clear and bright with no discharge of any kind; both eyes should be the same colour with no marks or flecks in them. If the third eyelid (in the front corner of the eye) is out it is a sign of stress. Ask yourself why is it stressed – lack of handling usually.

Ears - there should be no damage to the ears. Most nicks or cuts in ears, especially in English Lops, do not heal over completely. The ear should be clean and free from any waxing or sign of disease.

If you are buying an English Lop, ask to see the ears measured (length and width). Remember, an English Lop's ears stop growing at the age of 14 weeks (refer to the ear growth chart in Chapter 9).

For any other lop, if the ears are not set correctly (i.e. hanging close to the cheeks) there really is no simple answer. If they have enough width across the skull then they may well descend to the correct position in time, but similarly they may not. Again, a good look at both parents should tell what is likely to happen.

Front and Back legs - should be straight and strong. Turn the rabbit over on its back and look at the front feet; they should be clean, if the babies have been raised in good conditions. The pads should be well furred.

Check the inside of the front legs for any matting; rabbits use the inside of their front legs to wipe their noses, so any matting may indicate some nasal discharge.

Check the nails. Look for white toe nails; in a coloured rabbit this is a fault and if you intend to show or breed from the rabbit then it must be discarded, because it is an inherited trait and will therefore be passed on to its progeny.

Has it got all its toes and a dew claw with no deformities? Whilst the rabbit is on its back check the back legs and feet. If the baby is lying on its back in your hand then the back legs should lie parallel to the body. Check the toes and toe nails as for the front feet.

The genitals should be clean and free from any signs of disease. This is probably the first place where you will see signs of general ill health.

Sit the rabbit back on its feet, run your hands over its back. With your fingers feel along the ribs and up into the groin; there should be no lumps or irregularities. Look especially for a hernia, a small pea-like lump in the middle of the stomach.

Check the coat for bald patches or any infestation. Rabbit fleas are not uncommon and can usually be seen in the very thin fur around the ears or on the belly.

The tail should be straight with no kinks or breaks in it; run your fingers carefully up the tail and check for any irregularities.

If you intend to show or breed from the rabbit, carefully check the rabbit's colour. Chapter 15 describes the standard for each colour. Many colours are difficult to assess in a youngster, as for instance the banding required in the agouti family of rabbits does not appear until the rabbit matures.

Even a few white hairs in a self-coloured baby are not a good sign as they usually develop far more as they get older. Perhaps the best indication of the colour the baby is likely to mature into can be judged from its parents. A word of warning: an unscrupulous breeder may tell you any buck is the father of the baby and you cannot prove or disprove it. Colour is certainly very difficult to assess in a youngster and it is probably the one facet of the rabbit that you are going to have to trust the breeder on.

7. If you intend to show the rabbit it must have a British Rabbit Council ring on one of its back legs. It is the breeder's responsibility to fit the appropriate ring, but do check that it is the correct letter for the breed (see appropriate Breed Standard chapter) and is for the correct year. If you are buying a 'rung' rabbit then the breeder must give you a signed Transfer Card. When you have completed the Transfer Card you should send it, with the appropriate fee, to the BRC to have the registration transferred to your name.

8. If you are purchasing the rabbit with a view to showing it then you should have studied the appropriate Breed Standard before going to see the rabbit. It is also worthwhile spending some time at a show studying the winners; try to fix the look of the winners in your mind.

When you are in the breeder's rabbitry ask if you can 'pose' the rabbit (sit it in the position that breed sits on the show bench) and try to assess its qualities. This is not easy, especially if you have an experienced breeder breathing down your neck, but do not worry because it is exactly what they would do if they were looking at a rabbit with a view to buying it. No breeder is going to sell you his best rabbit, he has bred that for himself but you must be ruthless in your decision, because if you are not you will be stuck with a rabbit that never even gets placed. All rabbits go through a gangly stage, which is the period of maximum bone growth, from about 6 weeks to about 14 weeks and whilst they may look like a miniature version of the adult when about 4 weeks old this cannot be said for the period of bone growth. This must therefore be taken into consideration and makes the selecting of a potential winner all the more difficult.

9. It is against British Rabbit Council rules for a breeder to sell a baby rabbit under the age of 8 weeks, however even at 8 weeks old the kits are susceptible to stress related disorders and it is best not to buy a rabbit until it is about 12-14 weeks old, by which time it will be past the danger period for stress related disorders and should make a illness free transfer to your rabbitry.

10. The breeder should supply you with at least enough food for the rabbit for one week. This will allow you to gradually mix your food in with what the rabbit has been fed on so that the transition

does not bring on a stomach upset.

11. If you have not groomed or cut the nails on the breed of rabbit you are buying get the breeder to show you how to do it. Miniature Cashmere and Cashmere Lops need very different grooming to all the other lops. Similarly turning a full grown French or English Lop over to cut its nails is not for the faint hearted. Remember though that with the exception of the English Lop you are not allowed to cut the nails of an under 5 month lop if you intend to show it, so therefore you may have to make arrangements with the breeder to return when your rabbit is over 5 months old for a quick lesson in nail cutting. It is not difficult and is a skill every rabbit owner must learn.

12. Temperament - this can be very difficult to assess in a young lop as almost without exception they are all beautiful, loving bundles of fluff when young. So what can you do to assess the future temperament of the baby you wish to purchase? First of all, the older the kit is, the more likely it is that any behaviour problem will show itself. By the age of about 14 weeks then the young lop can be compared to a teenager, it is at this age that undesirable traits are likely to manifest themselves. So if you buy a very young rabbit, between 8 and 14 weeks then you really have no clue to future behaviour other than assessing the parents' temperament and watching the way the breeder handles his stock. Stock that has been well handled from a very young age by an experienced breeder will invariable develop into loving sociable adults.

In conclusion, the choosing of a young lop is very important no matter what you wish to do with it. With the exception of the big lops (French, English and Meissner) your baby may well live for up to ten years so be as particular as you like when choosing your lop; they are beautiful animals and their biggest failing is that they are exceptionally cute when young, but they are all cute so do not let your heart rule your head. If you want your lop as a pet you want a healthy animal, if you want it for showing you want a healthy rabbit that exhibits the qualities required by the Breed Standard.

Chapter 3
Housing Lops

BEFORE WE CAN DISCUSS the housing requirements of lops in detail we must consider the three separate reasons for keeping lops, namely; pet, house rabbit or show/breeding.

Pet lops are usually kept in small numbers and outside, house rabbits are invariably kept inside and often singularly, whereas show and breeding rabbits are 'usually' kept in some form of shed and often in very large numbers, up to 200 rabbits is not uncommon.

How you house your lop, or lops, will depend very much on which of these categories your lop(s) fall into as whilst each system is not necessarily mutually exclusive the system of housing you choose should reflect the lifestyle that you intend for your lop.

First we must consider what any rabbit housing has to provide because just like your own home there are certain basic common requirements that must be provided no matter what style of home is adopted.

Just like any of us in our home the rabbit must be safe and comfortable, it must live in a clean, dry, well ventilated, disease free environment. We are able to either take off or add extra clothing in order to maintain our bodies at a comfortable temperature and if this still does not achieve a satisfactory condition then we can open or close windows, turn heating up or down; but the rabbit that we have enclosed within an artificial space can do none of these. Therefore it is imperative that we consider how we can control the temperature within the animal's living environment.

Taking all of the above into consideration it can be seen that the choice of materials and the final construction to form housing for your lop, and the position where you place the rabbit's house, needs very careful consideration.

Housing Pet Lops

Owners of pet lops may well be seduced by the marketing and pricing of hutches that are sold in the pet shops across the country, however the majority of the commercially produced hutches in Britain are totally unsuitable for any lop to spend its entire life in. Invariably they are made of very thin plywood that neither keeps the wind or rain out nor will withstand the ingress of the lops' urine.

The other major fault in the majority of commercially sold hutches is the cheap, thin wire mesh that has too wide an opening allowing the rabbit to grip the wire with its teeth and all too often damage its teeth. It would appear that people who do not keep rabbits design these commercial hutches and that they are assembled by people whose sole intention is to make as large a profit as possible rather than provide the rabbit with a home that meets the basic requirements.

If you wish to house a pet lop you should be very careful in the choice of hutch as it will almost certainly spend the majority of its life in your garden resisting all the weather that the British climate can throw at it.

Before you even purchase your rabbit or hutch you must consider where you are going to position the hutch in the garden; it must not face the prevailing wind and it must not be exposed to the full summer sun.

Rabbits are natural burrowers so if you are going to buy a hutch with an attached run, which is ideal for the rabbit's well being, you will need to either dig a solid board at least nine inches down into the ground around the edge of the run or lay down some form of solid base, i.e. concrete slabs. This may not sound a very comfortable base for the rabbit to live on but is in fact ideal; it will not get muddy in the rain, the rabbit cannot dig into it and you can scrub it down and keep it clean and disease free.

So now that you have decided where to position the hutch (and maybe attached run) you can consider the hutch that will best meet the requirements of your lop.

Two simple guides are: purchase a hutch as big and as robust as possible. Size will obviously vary depending on which breed of lop you are going to acquire. A little Miniature Lop will live quite happily in a three foot hutch whilst an adult French or English Lop will require a six foot hutch that is at least two foot high and two foot deep.

Security is of paramount importance with any garden hutch. If there is any chance whatsoever that you have foxes in the area where you live then the hutch and wire must not only be very strong but should have a sheltered area where the rabbit can seek refuge, as even if the fox cannot break in to the hutch the rabbit may well die of fright if it is stuck in an exposed position faced with a fox trying to get

This run with shelter attached was designed by a fancier

at its dinner. All doors must have secure fasteners or even padlocks, to prevent them being opened accidentally or even accidentally not being closed correctly.

A pet rabbit's garden hutch will obviously have to be waterproof; this means a thick felt roof and good thick weatherboarding that will resist the ravages of the British climate. To assist in this weatherproofing the hutch roof should have a minimum of four inches of overhang at the front, this will shelter the open, wire mesh front and prevent the rain driving in. The hutch should be raised off the ground, preferably on legs, so as to prevent draughts and damp rising from the ground.

It is a fallacy that your rabbit will be cold living out in the garden; so long as they have plenty of dry straw to bed down in they will never be too cold and will be quite happy on the coldest of nights. Surprisingly it is the summer heat that is more dangerous. If the hutch is exposed to the midday sun then your rabbit can suffer untold discomfort trying to cope with high temperatures.

It is for this reason that it is better to have the run attached to the hutch, as your rabbit then has a chance to escape to the cooler inside of the hutch when it gets too hot out in the sun.

All too often people put the rabbit out in the (detached) run when they go off to work in the cool of the morning leaving the rabbit exposed, and trapped out in the full heat of the day, only to return home to find the rabbit suffering from heat exhaustion or worse, dead.

If for what ever reason you cannot have a run attached to the hutch and decide to have a separate free standing one, make sure that it has a sheltered end or that you put some form of cover over one end before you go off and leave your lop exposed out in what may become a death trap. If you do purchase a hutch with a run attached then do not be surprised to see your rabbit sat out in the rain or even snow; neither seem to bother them and even when they have the choice of going into a warm, dry hutch they will often sit outside in the worst of weather.

When buying a hutch great care should be taken to ensure that the wire mesh on the front is suitable, all too often it is not. The wire should be at least nineteen gauge and the holes should be one inch high by half an inch across. It is most important that the wire has been fitted this way round as often manufacturers will use the right wire but put it the other way round so that it is one inch across by half an inch high; they do this so as to use up the end of a roll and cut costs.

The reason why the wire must be fitted correctly is to prevent the rabbit getting its front teeth around it. Should a young lop gets its teeth around the wire and then pull and worry at it, as they have a tendency to do, permanent damage may be done to the teeth. Because rabbits' teeth continually grow and are aligned so that they naturally wear each other down as they chew, any accidental damage that misaligns them will prevent this natural wearing down process.

Should this happen the teeth will just continue to grow and will require regular trimming by a veterinary surgeon. This will mean that the rabbit has a life of discomfort, and you have a life of veterinary bills. It can therefore be seen why the importance of having the correct wire fitted in the correct manner from the outset cannot be overstated. If you are going to purchase a run, either attached or free-standing, then the same rules must apply to the wire the run is made of.

I have already stated that the majority of commercially produced hutches were almost certainly designed by people who do not keep rabbits and the fitting of a divider to create a 'sleeping compartment' must be the proof of this if any were needed. Most rabbits will not sleep in the enclosed 'sleeping compartment' but instead use it as a toilet area. The dividing board in the hutch does give the rabbit somewhere to shelter should a particularly strong wind spring up from an unusual direction or rain drive into the hutch, but a sleeping compartment it is not. Having said that, it is better to have the divider fitted, but it is certainly not essential and its presence or absence should not sway the purchase of a hutch.

Before you decide which hutch to buy have a good look at the floor inside of it; if you intend to keep a buck in the hutch you will find that because they are clean animals they always use the same corner for a toilet. This means that the corner can become very wet and if the hutch is constructed of thin plywood then it will very quickly rot rendering the hutch useless.

Doe rabbits are much dirtier in their toilet habits and tend to churn their bedding, this means that their waste products are continually mixed with the bedding so that although the bedding gets dirty quicker, and therefore needs changing more often, the net effect is that you do not get one very wet corner.

If you can buy a hutch that not only has a very thick floor but also has some kind of bitumen coating on it then it should last many years even if a buck is kept in it.

I have also mentioned that you should buy a hutch that is constructed of thick, strong weatherboarding because of its suitability to keep the wind and rain out. However, there is also another very valuable asset to this type of construction in its ability to resist the gnawing that it may well receive from the rabbit. Some rabbits never gnaw their hutch, however, others seem to be at it all the time and if you do happen to get a gnawer then a thin plywood hutch will not last two minutes.

So although you may think that you can either knock up a hutch from a few scraps of wood and a bit of wire or nip down to your local superstore there is in fact a great deal to consider if you want to provide your pet lop with the basic requirements of a secure, clean, dry, disease free environment.

Housing House or Semi House Lops

House rabbits have become very popular in recent years and are kept in one of two ways; either as a semi-house rabbit, i.e. having a fairly traditional hutch outside the house in which it lives when you are not able to give it your full attention and then having the run of the house whilst you are able to keep an eye on it, or alternatively having some kind of indoor hutch that it can be shut into for safety and then let out to roam the house.

The semi-house rabbit would obviously use a normal hutch as described above for any pet lop. However, it might be worth considering a hutch where the door could be left open so that the rabbit could come and go as it pleases; this will mean either a ramp up in to the hutch or short legs so that the rabbit can hop in and out when you choose to leave the door open. Leaving access to the hutch means that your lop can get to its food and water whenever it

This indoor hutch is of good size but should be provided with a ramp

wants and also seek refuge whenever it wants.

The ability for your lop to be able to seek refuge when 'it' wants is a vital consideration when choosing an indoor rabbit cage. If you allow your lop free unrestricted access to your house twenty four hours a day there is no doubt it will wreck the house in no time at all and may well harm itself as well. It is therefore vital that you have a large, safe indoor cage where you can secure your rabbit for its own good as well as the good of your house. The golden rule is that no rabbit should ever be left loose in the house when you are not there to supervise it.

There are many designs of indoor cage on the market, most are brightly coloured and look great at first sight but as none is cheap it is quite important that you make the right choice first time and are not just taken in by the flashy appearance. Think about the eventual size of your little baby lop (check the size of each breed of lop in the appropriate chapter), a small cage may look fine for a little baby French or English Lop but an adult lop weighing 12 – 15lbs. needs a very large space if it is to be confined all day whilst you are out at work and then again all night while you are sleeping. Not only has the animal to sleep in the cage but it must also have a food bowl, water bottle, hayrack and toys to prevent boredom.

Returning to our basic requirement for housing it will be recalled that safety for the lop is of paramount importance and this is never more so than for the house rabbit; the lop must be secured from other pets and children. If you are going to leave your lop in its cage in the house with other pets then you must ensure that there is absolutely no way that a cat or dog could break in to the cage although it is better if you can ensure that the rabbit is left in a different room from all other pets because even if dogs or cats can not break-in their worrying at the cage could cause enormous stress on the rabbit that is confined with nowhere to go. Remember, it is the rabbit's natural instinct to take flight and run for cover at the first sign of danger and just as before in the fox situation the rabbit may actually die from the stress induced by an attack on its living quarters if it has nowhere to hide.

Looking at the indoor cages on the market you will see that many only have a top opening, this type of cage is not really appropriate as when the lop is out and free in the house it should still have access to its food and water, which is usually in the cage, therefore a side opening door will allow the lop freedom to come and go and access its food and water as it pleases.

Most indoor cages on the market are made of plastic and these are ideal as they can easily be cleaned and kept hygienic, however, many of the plastic cages have smooth floors that may be ideal for cleaning but rabbits simply cannot hold their feet on a smooth plastic floor and the poor lop may well spend its time in the cage unable to stand or even sit up as its feet just keep sliding from under it.

It may cause a slight problem in your house but you really should put a layer of shaving in the bottom of the indoor cage. The problem caused by the lop scattering some of the shavings when they come out of the cage is nothing compared to the trouble you could inadvertently cause if you put newspaper on the cage floor.

Rabbits physically do not have the ability to cough or be sick and therefore anything they eat must pass through the body. When chewed-up newspaper mixes with the digestive juices in the gut it does not break down, but rather, it forms a ball and can cause a compacted gut that will often have to be removed by costly surgery and will always cause the lop enormous pain and distress.

For a related reason you may consider that a cage that has solid plastic sides rather than plastic covered wire bars is better; the solid sides will prevent a small child poking things into the cage that the rabbit may then eat causing a impacted gut. The solid sides will also alleviate the teeth problems that were discussed previously in relation to the wire on outdoor cages.

If you do decide on a cage with solid sides then you must think carefully about where you are going to position the cage. All the solid sided cages have a grill on the top for access and ventilation but obviously the air flow will not be as great as in an open sided cage. Whilst you can easily position the cage out of direct sunlight so that it does not overheat, it is when the central heating is turned up high in the winter that the poor lop could inadvertently be trapped in an enclosed space that is far too hot for it.

The ideal temperature for rabbits is 16° C. This is a fairly low temperature for most houses these days as people tend to keep their central heating set at about 18° - 20° C and certainly on a cold winter's evening when all the doors and windows are closed and the heating is turned fully up then temperatures well in excess of 20° C are the norm in most houses. It can therefore be seen that the positioning of the indoor cage is quite important if your lop is to lead a comfortable life in your house. The consequence of a lop living for prolonged periods in temperatures above 16° C are that it will be in permanent moult.

Before leaving the housing requirements of the house rabbit it must be mentioned that the reverse of the over heating problem discussed above, namely draughts, must be avoided at all costs. Rabbits no more like living in a draught than we do and a cage sited where there is a permanent draught may well cause the lop to have runny eyes or worse, to contract snuffles, which is a serious respiratory disorder causing the rabbit much distress as it continually sneezes as it tries to clear its nasal passages of a thick white mucus.

Housing Show and Breeding Lops

For numerous reasons show lops are invariably kept under some form of cover, perhaps the most obvious reason for this is that the cover gives you, the rabbit keeper, protection from the vagaries of

the British climate and this is
very important when you keep
a lot of rabbits, especially if
you work, and therefore have
to clean out a lot of rabbits on
a specific day whether you like
it or not. It is no fun at all in
the winter when it is pouring
with rain or freezing cold and
snowing and you have fifty or
even a hundred or more hutches to clean out.

A typical rabbit shed

Show rabbits should not live outside where they will be exposed
to natural sunlight, as the sun will 'turn' their coats. This means that
a black or blue rabbit will acquire a rusty tinge and become
unshowable; it is not only the self-coloured lops that the light will
affect, it will not do any colour any good.

Keeping the rabbits under cover can mean a variety of things.
For most people it will mean adapting what you have got, unless
you are already a committed fancier who is moving house and then
you will almost certainly be looking for a house that has the ideal
facility for your rabbits.

Many people make use of a carport as this meets the first two
requirements: shelter for you and protection from the sun. Although
clearly there could be security problems in preventing other animals
coming in and worrying your stock, and may well allow easy access
for people.

However, by far the most popular set up is to use a 'shed'. This
may in fact be just that, a wooden shed, or it may be a converted
out-building or garage but in the language of the fancier it is always
called the 'shed' in Britain (in the U.S.A. it is known as the 'barn').

If you are going to set up a rabbit shed then you must return to
the basic requirements: safe, comfortable, clean, dry, well ventilated
and disease free.

Safety for you means that you can secure your rabbits, as you are
likely to have a lot of very valuable stock in the shed and you must
know that it is secure when you are not around; on more than one
occasion fanciers have had their sheds broken into and stock stolen.

So whether it is padlocks, security alarms or video cameras you must make sure that your huge investment in time and money is protected from unwanted intruders. Safety for your rabbits means that they are protected from attack by other animals or, unfortunately, human beings. This means taking measures to prevent the entry of other pet animals and unwanted humans. During the hot summer months you will almost certainly want all the doors and windows open and must therefore fit security screens to all openings.

Perhaps the most taxing problem when setting up a new rabbit shed is ventilation. In the cold, wet and windy winter months you will want to close the shed down to keep it dry and maintain the temperature, but in doing so you are reducing the flow of fresh air and the noxious gases emitted from the rabbits and condensation will soon build up. This is a recipe for disaster; disease will soon take hold and spread rapidly throughout your stock.

Conversely, in the hot summer months, sheds can heat up very quickly, especially when the weather is very hot and there is little or no wind to aid airflow; rabbits do not like hot conditions and can die of heatstroke. So ventilation must be the prime concern. Positioning the shed under a large deciduous tree in a shaded area of the garden will help because the tree will have leaves in the summer and provide shade during the heat of the day, whereas, it will be leaf free during the cool winter months and not restrict what little heat there is to be had. A wooden shed will almost certainly need the assistance of fans in the summer to reduce the heat, therefore you should consider providing mains electricity when you are erecting the shed. If you can position the shed so that it is not in line with the prevailing wind then you can probably get away with having no glass in the windows, this will greatly aid air flow and so long as the window openings have well fitting fly screens securely attached then you should be able to make the rabbits' lives far more comfortable. For your own comfort the mains electricity can give you lighting in the shed, enabling you to work in the shed on dark winter evenings and also apply some gentle heating on the coldest of winter days even if it is only for you on cleaning out days.

If you are setting up a new shed to house show rabbits then there is an almost cast iron rule – make it as big as you can to house as many rabbits as possible because almost certainly in no time at all you will find that you have run out of space and are looking at ways to expand your set up.

Within the shed the most economical way to house a lot of rabbits is in blocks of hutches. There are numerous specialists who will build blocks of hutches that fit together and therefore make the most of the space available. However, their construction is not beyond the average handy man. Anyone contemplating such a venture would be advised to visit a few other sheds and study how others have done it.

Because your show lops are going to live their entire life in their hutches the hutches must be big enough. A Miniature Lop will need a three foot hutch whilst the large French and English Lops will need six foot hutches and obviously the intermediate size lops will need a hutch somewhere between the two extremes. It is normal practice to have larger breeding pens as a doe with a rapidly growing litter will need more space than a resting doe. It can therefore be seen that careful consideration must not only be given to the size and mix of hutches but of course the shed that the hutches will fit into.

Whilst the blocks of hutches within a shed do not require the same weatherproofing as the hutches of the pet rabbit that stand outside it is still advisable to construct the blocks of hutches from strong materials. The rabbits will spend their entire lives in the hutches and some rabbits can be quite destructive; the use of cheap materials will almost certainly increase the chance of the rabbit

Indoor hutch under construction

causing itself harm and lead to a continuous repair programme. There really is no point in starting off with cheap, inferior blocks of hutches and it would be better to buy fewer better quality blocks than it would be to fill the shed with cheap ones that will need replacing within a short space of time.

The blocks of hutches in which you house your show lops must have many of the features that I have discussed for the pet lop's housing, particularly the wire on the front of the pen; it is most important that the correct gauge (19 gauge) wire with the correct opening, one inch high by half an inch wide is used. There is absolutely no requirement for sleeping compartments in show lops blocks of hutches, but the floor and an inch or so up the walls should be covered in a bitumen sealant to prevent urine soaking into the floor and running into the hutch below.

Under construction: a block of hutches for medium sized lops. Note the use of litter boards

One feature that most fanciers have fitted in their hutches is the 'litter board', this is a three to four inch piece of wood that is fitted below the bottom of the opening door so that when the door is opened the board remains in place and retains the shavings and bedding. You will spend a considerable amount of time sweeping and tidying your shed so any small features like litter boards that are fitted when the blocks are constructed will save you much time and energy in the long run.

It may seem whimsical, but most fanciers have a radio in their shed and there is in fact a very good reason for this. By enclosing your show lops in a shed you are in fact cutting off all the normal stimuli that the garden-housed pet rabbit would be exposed to. The general comings and goings in the garden, even the birds and bees all create interest for the garden rabbit and of course there will be a variety of sounds, many just routine ones, such as distant traffic but they all become part of the garden rabbit's life.

Lops enclosed in a shed are cut off from much of this and therefore a radio tuned to a station that has music and talk can at least provide some aural stimulus. Rabbits that live in a completely sound free environment are highly likely to become very distressed and agitated when exposed to sudden noise – as in taking a lop to a rabbit show that is both busy and noisy. Therefore the radio in the shed is not such a joke after all and is in fact a very important part of the overall environment that you provide for your lops.

If you are lucky enough to be setting up a new shed and you are considering all of the above features then it would be worth adding one last consideration – water. You will need fresh water for your lops and to wash your bottles and food bowls so if you can have running water and drainage at your shed then you will not only make your life easier but be the envy of all the other fanciers who have to carry their water from the house and all their food bowls and bottles to the house for cleaning. It is a luxury but if you can build it into your design you will not regret it.

Rabbits are creatures of habit and having set up a comfortable, safe, dry, well ventilated, disease free environment for them you must now establish routines for their feeding and maintenance in order to keep them happy and healthy.

Above: a block of two hutches designed for a French Lop. The firm that makes these purpose-built hutches displays at leading shows in the south of England

Chapter 4
Maintaining Lops

Young French Lop. A balanced diet is essential if you are to maintain your lop in optimum health

I T really does not matter if your lops have come from the best breeder in the land and are the best lops that money can buy – if you cannot look after them properly and keep to a regular maintenance regime they will lead a short, miserable life bringing you nothing but heartache and veterinary bills.

The lops in our care are totally dependent on us literally for their lives so we all have what is called 'a duty of care'. This duty of care requires us, like all animal keepers, to comply with the principles behind the 'Five Freedoms'. Experts throughout the world to assess animal welfare use these five freedoms:

Freedom from Hunger and Thirst

Freedom from Discomfort

Freedom from Pain, Injury and Disease

Freedom from Fear and Distress

Freedom to express Normal Behaviour

Rabbits are creatures of habit and as such require us, their keepers, to provide everything they require to comply with the Five Freedoms.

Having provided a safe, dry, well ventilated environment for your lop as described in Chapter 3 it is now up to you, the lop's keeper, to provide bedding, food and water, to keep the hutch clean and disease free and to maintain the lop's health by regular health checks, by grooming and by regularly trimming its nails and by regular vaccination against endemic parasitic diseases.

Water - Rabbits can drink without eating but they cannot eat without drinking; it is therefore absolutely essential that all your stock is provided with clean, easily accessible drinking water at all times.

There is nothing wrong with using the tap water in Britain, although the quality of the water may vary around the country your rabbits will very quickly adapt to it. So if you have moved your lops from one area to another you need not worry as it is unlikely to upset them unless they are very young, in which case it may well be advisable to bring water from the original home of the baby lop so that it is one less stress factor that you are imposing on it.

If you are taking lops to shows when the weather is hot or they are to stay overnight you are required to supply water for them so it is as well to take water from home so that you do not add an additional stress to what is already an exceedingly stressful situation for any rabbit.

There are three ways that you can make water available to your lop; in a water bowl, in a bottle or by an automatic drinking system. Before considering the merits of each system it is worth noting that the drinking or rather the non-drinking of water is an excellent indicator of your lop's health. It therefore follows that if in the evening you check a water bottle that you know you filled with fresh water in the morning and find that there has been 'no movement' (i.e. the water has not gone down at all) then the lop clearly has not received any water. This may be because of a fault in the bottle or because there is something wrong with the lop and it is not drinking. Making water available in a bowl or by an automatic system takes away this wonderful indicator of health.

Drinking bowls have the disadvantage that rabbits will almost certainly either kick them or deposit dropping and shavings in the water, therefore the water would need to be checked and changed at regular (every few hours) intervals.

These are the disadvantages of using water bowls, however they do have one big advantage. If a rabbit does not drink from its bottle and you suspect it to be ill then the very first thing to do is to put a bowl of water in the hutch as they will often make the effort to drink from a bowl when drinking from a bottle is too much effort.

Any rabbit suffering from diarrhoea will very quickly dehydrate and must have fluids to prevent it spiralling towards death so a water bowl makes it easier for the sick rabbit to drink and if you add dioralyte to the water it will help replace essential elements that the rabbit is losing.

It is easy to get the rabbit that has never seen a water bowl in its life to drink from it; if you put your hand on the back of the lop's head and gently and briefly dunk its nose in the water (this may sound cruel but is a very quick action that literally wets the lop's lips) it will come out licking its lips and have realised that is what the bowl is for. If you are quick enough to notice that your lop is not drinking from its bottle and can get it drinking from a water bowl

then you may well avert a
potential disaster.

The majority of rabbit
keepers use the standard
'bunny bottle' that is
available from every pet
shop, they work well, are
readily available and
cheap.

Perhaps the only fault
with the bunny bottle is that
it is not very strong; it
breaks easily if dropped
and some rabbits seem to
master getting their teeth
through the wire and
nipping the edge of it,
which means all the water
leaks out, the rabbit gets no
water and the bottle has to
be thrown away. If you are

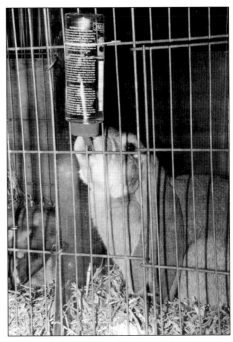

"Bunny bottle" in use at a rabbit show

unlucky enough to have a rabbit that masters this trick then the only
thing to do is to buy a bung and spout (from specialist dealer) and
use a glass (milk) bottle.

It is obviously very time consuming to fill a lot of bottles every
day; this time can be significantly reduced if you fit a 'spring'
(available from specialist dealers only) to the cage wire. With the
spring fitted you can easily and quickly lift the bottle out and refit it
once filled.

Plastic water bottles will quickly accumulate a thin layer of algae
if they are not cleaned regularly. Whilst a bottle brush will do the
job, a much quicker and easy way of cleaning a plastic water bottle
is to put a half inch of water in it and then a length of sink plug
chain (without the plug), place your thumb over the top of the bottle
and shake vigorously. The chain will act as a scourer and clean right
into all the corners.

The more lops you keep the longer it will take each day to clean and fill every rabbit's bottle and you may want to consider an automatic watering system. This is a system of tubes that feed to each individual hutch from a header tank. Each lop has a nipple on a one-way valve so that the water is supplied on demand.

This system has many advantages, time being the biggest one, and you could supply an additive in the water and know that each rabbit would get it at exactly the same strength.

If you are away at a show and someone else is looking after your rabbits it is one less thing for them to worry about, as you know the rabbits have a permanent mains supply of fresh water. Of course, its biggest failing is that you lose that valuable health check, you just have no way of knowing whether an individual lop has drunk or not.

Food – Like us all, rabbits should be fed according to their lifestyle, so the sedentary rabbit that leads a quiet life in its hutch will clearly need less food or a lower nutritional feed than the active rabbit that is growing, running around a lot, showing, breeding or raising young.

Perhaps the biggest failing in feeding rabbits is 'ad lib' feeding, where the animal is allowed to help itself from a full bowl that is continually topped up.

This method of feeding allows the rabbit to 'selectively feed' i.e. it just picks out its favourite pieces and does not have the complete diet that the food was designed to deliver.

Obesity, the inability to groom itself and a range of dental problems are usually attributed to this method of feeding, as is the horrific 'fly strike'.

Fly strike can attack a rabbit very quickly in hot weather; if the rabbit has diarrhoea and is overweight through poor or an incorrect diet it physically cannot clean itself and flies will be attracted to the dirty area. The flies will lay their eggs in the dirty matted fur and when it is hot the eggs will quickly hatch and the resulting maggots will burrow into the skin of the rabbit.

If this sounds disgusting the sight of it is even worse, so one can only imagine what pain the poor animal must be suffering and all this suffering can so easily be caused by owners being 'too kind' and overfeeding, spoiling with treats and allowing the rabbit to selectively feed.

Whilst you may think you are being kind to the rabbit by making sure it always has food available you are in fact almost certainly causing the lop problems even if they do not materialise until later in its life. Rabbits naturally eat in the evening and early morning and therefore it is best to feed them their daily ration in the early evening and then take their food bowl away in the morning.

Your lop is confined to its hutch and it cannot graze when it feels like it; therefore, it is best to give a handful of hay when you take the empty bowl away in the morning as this gives the lop something to chew on throughout the day.

Hay is an essential part of the rabbits' diet for a variety of reasons, perhaps the most important is that the grinding action required to chew the hay helps maintain the teeth. Rabbits teeth grow continually throughout their lives and require the chewing of long fibrous material to keep them at their 'normal' length. Indigestible fibre (hay) is also required by the gut and is an important part of the complete diet of the rabbit. To use this method of feeding you must know what the daily requirement of your lop is.

Many pet owners fear that they will under feed their lops, and consequently end up over feeding them. A miniature lop requires just two ounces of mix a day, whilst a young, active French or English lop may well eat about eight ounces of the same mix daily.

The only real way to ascertain an individual lop's food requirements is by observation. If there is still food remaining from the previous feed then clearly you are over feeding; if your lop empties its bowl within a few minutes of being fed and is always up pawing at its cage wire whenever you are in the vicinity then perhaps you need to increase the ration.

The fibre content of the food is very important and you should look for a food with a high fibre content (18 –20% is considered high). The protein requirement should be varied with the lops' life style; a sedentary lop will maintain a healthy condition if fed on a low protein food (10 –12%) whereas, a lactating doe will need a much higher protein content (16-18%).

One way to avoid selective eating and its problems is to feed pellets; whilst they may not look attractive to us if they are fed along with good quality hay they contain all the nutrients that the lop requires and therefore the complete diet is always eaten.

In recent years there has been an enormous rise in the sale of rabbit 'treats' in our pet shops; attractively packaged, most are deliberately priced so as to be in the child's pocket money range.

As 'interest toys' these treats do a good job in entertaining the rabbit and giving the bored hutch-bound rabbit something to do, but, as part of the lop's diet they are all completely superfluous, and can in fact be as harmful as lots of sweets are to children; not only can they rot their teeth but also fill them up so that they do not eat their correct food.

In times gone by it was quite common to make up a large proportion of the rabbits' diet with wild herbage collected from the fields and hedgerows but unfortunately this is no longer practical in most parts of Britain.

So much of Britain is now urbanised and those areas that are not, are criss-crossed with road and rail networks, all of which pollute the vegetation that surrounds them. Even those rural areas that remain, are in general farmed using such intensive farming methods that the surrounding herbage will be polluted with all manner of chemicals.

So whilst it is unlikely that you can collect sufficiently large amounts of wild herbs to supplement your lops' diet it is quite possible to 'cultivate' a wild area within your garden that will provide you with unpolluted wild herbs that can be used as nutritional treats that will do your lop far more good than shop bought treats.

A further consideration about the feeding of your lop is what you are going to put the food in. To

store the food it should be kept in an airtight, vermin-proof container.

To feed your lop you should use a heavy ceramic bowl; plastic bowls are certainly of no use whatsoever as rabbits chew and destroy them. If you put the food in too small a bowl the lop will either stand on one rim and tip it over, often burying its day's ration of food beneath the upturned bowl, or pick it up in its teeth and throw it around the hutch.

This may not in itself be a problem other than to you when you are trying to find the bowl buried below the bedding, but may be the cause of damage to the teeth and will certainly be noisy – usually during the night!!

Bedding – If you are intending to keep a lot of lops then bedding becomes an important issue; it is bulky, heavy, expensive and has to be disposed of after the lops have dirtied it and finished with it.

In Britain we tend to keep our rabbits in wooden hutches and bed them on wood shavings; this is not the case throughout the world, particularly in the U.S.A. where it is the normal practice to keep them in single layer wire cages suspended above the ground so that the rabbits' urine and droppings fall to the ground below.

In the majority of cases our wood shaving system is absolutely ideal; the shavings are readily available in pet and farm shops, they are clean and disease free, they are comfortable for the rabbit, they are absorbent and they do not irritate or cause the rabbit any distress.

The down side is that they are not particularly cheap. They are bulky and difficult to transport and if you have a lot of lops then the amount of dirty shavings you have to dispose of every week can be quite a problem. They do not burn without creating an enormous amount of smoke; they do not rot, unless mixed with a lot of green organic matter; most council dustmen will not take them away and contrary to what you may see written (usually in American books) worms will not eat them.

So keeping large numbers of lops can create a big problem just in disposing of the waste that they will generate. There is no easy answer and every lop keeper has to find their own solution, but it is a problem that every lop keeper must be aware of before they take any lops into their home.

For some reason many people feel that they can either keep lops on shredded newspaper or that they should put a layer of newspaper underneath the shavings to absorb the excess moisture.

Both of these are an absolute no-no as not only will the lop have permanently black feet from the ink but on a more serious note, rabbits do not have the ability to be sick therefore everything they eat must pass completely through the digestive system and out the other end.

If you put newspaper in a lop's hutch it will chew it, however when the chewed up newspaper gets into the gut and mixes with the gastric juices it will form a solid ball that cannot be passed and causes what is known as a impacted gut. If this is diagnosed and operated on early enough the lop may be saved but many rabbits die in agony from this owner-induced problem.

So a deep (2-3inches) layer of clean white wood shavings changed on a regular basis is quite sufficient to provide the comfort required for normal living. When housing large lops (French and English) it is best to add a further layer of good quality barley straw on top of the shavings to add bulk and prevent the lop getting sore hocks as the sheer weight of the animal means that the hocks will press through the shavings and the lop's hocks will be permanently in contact with the wooden boards.

Lops that live permanently outdoors will be quite happy living on shavings; however, in the really cold depths of winter good quality barley straw can be added to add warmth to the bedding. As long as the bedding and straw is dry then the lop will be able to keep itself warm and it only becomes a problem if the bedding is allowed to get wet and then freezes. No rabbit can be comfortable if it is outside on a freezing cold night and has to sit on frozen bedding.

Shavings are obviously easy to store. As long as they are kept dry they will be ok; however hay and straw can be a breeding ground for disease if it is not stored correctly. In the hot summer weather hay and straw will sweat if kept enclosed, especially in plastic bags in the sunlight. This sweating will cause micro-organisms in the hay/straw to breed and multiply.

Well-kept hay/straw should have 'a nose' to it, i.e. it should smell sweet whereas poorly kept hay/straw would have a musty smell.   If musty hay/straw is put into the lop's hutch it is highly likely to infect the hutch and the lop. The use of musty hay/straw is the main cause of fur mites in rabbits.

You must insist that all the hay and straw that you buy is of the highest quality and 'fresh' when you obtain it. Hay should have been cut for at least six months before it is used – which may seem rather strange when we talk of fresh hay – six month old hay will have lost its greenness and have that lovely 'nose' to it.

To keep hay/straw correctly it should be removed from plastic bags and placed in a sack that should then be suspended so as to allow a free flow of air around it.

If you live in a urban area where sacks are not everyday items then you will find that your local pet shop will usually give you one as the peanuts they buy for resale for wild birds come in sacks that they throw away once they have sold the peanuts.

There are other beddings on the market such as medi-bed and a balm-scented shaving/straw mixture; however, they are generally more expensive, less readily available and offer no real benefits over shavings. Occasionally you may come across shredded paper bedding being sold in bulk - this really should be avoided for rabbits as it goes to the newspaper problem of impacting the gut.

Hutch Cleaning and Cleanliness – it is absolutely imperative that your lop lives in a disease-free environment and the only way that this can be achieved is by good husbandry.

It was stated early in this chapter that rabbits are creatures of habit and a regular routine applies just as much to cleaning as it does to feeding and watering.

In the majority of cases bucks are cleaner than does. Most bucks will use the same corner of their hutch as a toilet area and keep the remainder of their hutch very clean, whereas does tend not to have a designated toilet area and mess anywhere in their hutch.

Added to the doe's general untidiness is the habit that does have of churning their bedding. This has the effect of mixing the soiled bedding in with any that is still clean, thus making it all dirty.

Of course there are exceptions to this general rule and you may be lucky and get a clean doe; similarly you may be unlucky and get a dirty buck.

In the case of the 'normal' clean buck it may be quite practical to clean out the 'dirty corner' every few days and turn some of the clean bedding into his toilet area, then top up his clean area with some fresh shavings. In this case it would be quite acceptable to strip the hutch out completely and disinfect it only every couple of weeks.

In the case of the 'normal doe' you will almost certainly have to completely empty the hutch at least once a week, thoroughly disinfect it and use completely new bedding.

Show bucks and does with litters will obviously need cleaning more regularly. It is no good allowing a show lop to get dirty and then having to spend hours getting it clean for a show; it should live permanently in a clean environment.

In the case of the doe with a litter, the doe will be eating and drinking more than normal and therefore making more waste. As the kittens grow they will add to the waste. This waste is a breeding ground for disease, disease that of course the young kits are highly susceptible to.

So just how do you clean out a lop's hutch? Some basic equipment should be kept especially for the purpose. A strong dustpan and stiff brush, a paint scraper and a disinfectant spray are all that are required. The lop should be removed from its hutch and placed somewhere safe.

The waste should be cleared from the hutch with the dustpan and brush and put into plastic bags and sealed immediately. It should then be removed from the vicinity of the rabbit's hutch and disposed of as soon as possible.

When the hutch is empty the paint scraper can be used to get any mess out of the corners or to remove any droppings that might have got trodden into the floor and dried hard. The hutch should then be thoroughly sprayed with a strong disinfectant; it is best to spray onto the walls of the hutch and allow the disinfectant to run down into the floor/wall join.

The hutch should then be left to dry before putting the new bedding in as the disinfectant will be rendered useless if the new bedding is put onto it whilst it is still wet.

Once the new bedding is in the hutch the lop can be returned to the hutch; it is best to put some food in when you return the lop as this will prevent it leaving uneaten caecotrophes (the natural soft droppings that the rabbit will normally eat) and then treading them into the clean, fresh bedding.

On a less frequent basis you should consider a thorough spring-clean of the hutches and surrounding areas, where everything is removed, all surfaces are thoroughly scrubbed with bleach and then repainted.

Of course the more lops you keep the bigger this job becomes but it really should be done at least once a year, usually as a spring clean following the rabbit shed being shut down for winter.

Maintaining a **disease free environment** for your lops to live in has to include all the areas that they impinge on. This means inside the hutch, its surrounding area and any runs they may use. This can be very difficult as the enemies are numerous and therefore your defences may need to be quite complex.

Attack from airborne predators is perhaps the most difficult to defend against. Whilst we can put fine mesh nets over all the doors and windows in a rabbitry and use a variety of fly killers and zappers to eliminate those that do get through and are big enough to see with the eye, many diseases are carried as micro-organisms and therefore cannot be stopped by nets or eliminated by sprays and the like. These micro-organisms are so hard to defend against that in fact the only practical way to ensure against attack by them is to accept that they will be there and vaccinate against the diseases they may bring with them.

But just how can you defend against flies and the like if you keep your lops outside? Of course you can place netting over the wire front to the hutch but this will almost certainly not eliminate all attackers and the only thing that you can do is to keep the lop and the hutch scrupulously clean so that there is no odour there to attract flies.

Disease-carrying rodents are without doubt a major enemy of rabbit keepers and must be excluded from the rabbit's environment at all costs. The rabbit's food must be stored in an airtight, vermin proof, container; this will usually mean a dustbin kept especially for it. If you decide to keep a lot of lops then you must be prepared to take the measures, as unpleasant as they may be, required to eliminate absolutely all rodents.

At the very first sign of rodents in the vicinity of your lops you must take action; in fact it is better to take preventative measures before you see their signs, especially in early autumn when they will be looking for a warm comfortable home for the winter.

There can be no doubt that the best defence against any disease carrier is cleanliness of the lop, its hutch and its surroundings. Cleanliness can only be achieved by regular, thorough, routine maintenance.

Your routine maintenance schedule should include **Health Checks** on your lop and these can be built into your everyday routine. Your daily health check is so simple that you may not realise you have done it, yet it can save the life of a sick animal.

The water bottle check is absolutely vital: fill the bottle - full, everyday. If there is no movement on the bottle i.e. it is still full when you next feed, you have a problem.

Of course your first check should be to make sure that the bottle is actually working. This is easily done by giving the bottle a shake and then squeezing it to make sure a fine jet of water comes from the spout. If the bottle is working then you must assume that the lop has not drunk and if this is the case then it is potentially a very serious situation.

Your first reaction should be to remove the lop from its hutch and check it over to see if you can identify the reason. If you cannot see anything wrong then it is best to put a bowl of water in the hutch, dunking the lop's head in the water (as described earlier) to wet its lips.

The second daily check is the lop's food bowl. If the lop has not eaten its food from the previous feed then it is an indication that something may be wrong. This indication is not necessarily one to worry about as it is not unusual for a rabbit to miss a feed and as long as it is drinking then it can go several days without food without any long term effect.

However, it is worrying for the owner and it is obviously not a situation that you want to let develop, so you may well try to tempt the non-eating lop with a tasty treat; parsley is particularly good for getting them going again.

The third and final check is the lop itself. On a daily basis it is sufficient to take in the lop's general disposition. Is it up at the front of the hutch waiting to be fed? Is it sat in the corner of the hutch facing the wall? The observant keeper of lops will soon notice when there is something amiss.

A full health check should be carried out at least once a week and usually on cleaning-out day. This is really a very

Cutting nails of a Miniature Lop (Photo Lea Fletcher)

simple routine; it is what every judge does when he first checks out a rabbit as he begins to judge it. Watching a judge, you may not think that all these points are being checked but of course the experienced judge does it very quickly and proficiently.

Take the lop from its hutch and place it on a solid non-slip surface. Starting at the front of the animal check its nose and eyes for any discharge. Check that the teeth have not been damaged. Look inside its ears for any discharge or foreign bodies and then run the ear between your fingers checking for any lumps, bumps or cuts.

With the lop sat on the table run your hands over its back feeling for anything untoward, then bring your hands back from the tail to the head rolling the coat as you go. As you do so look carefully at the undercoat and check for anything that should not be there; flaky skin, any creepies like fleas.

English Lop with Mikki groomer

Now turn the lop upside down and check its feet and legs. If the nails need cutting - cut them – do not put it off. If you have not cut rabbits nails' before it is best to get an experienced fancier to teach you how to do it as no written description can adequately explain what is a simple process (except on French and English Lops – a job for an experienced handler).

If the lop is a show rabbit and is wearing a BRC ring then whilst it is still upside down check that the ring still turns freely and has no foreign matter stuck under it. Finally check the sexual organs, anus and tail; all should be clean and free from any signs of disease.

If your lop has weight limits when being shown (see chapters 7 – 14 for each breed's specific weights) then now is the time to weigh the lop. If you show your lops then you should invest in a suitable set of scales especially for this purpose, but even if you only keep lops as pets then it is still well worthwhile keeping a regular check on their weight.

Having carried out this thorough health check you can now place the lop somewhere secure whilst you clean out the hutch.

With the exception of the two cashmere breeds, **Grooming** of lops is not an arduous task and requires only the minimum of specialist equipment but it is a task that should be carried out on a regular basis to keep the lop in the peak of condition.

All rabbits moult, this is a natural part of their life cycle and whilst many breeders have special concoctions to try to speed up the process, you cannot stop it.

The moulting process will first be noticed on one of your weekly health checks and when you roll the coat, instead of seeing the skin below the fur you will notice a new layer of hair growing. It is usually seen on the shoulders first, it often looks like a dark shadow and can be quite concerning to the new rabbit owner who has never seen it before.

There just is no answer to how long it takes any rabbit to clear its moult; many experienced breeders will deliberately breed from 'lines' that they know are quick moulters, but it can take anything from a month to six months.

Many rabbits get 'stuck in the moult', which means that they clear the coat on the back and then as the moult works its way down the sides it just seems to stop and you are then left with a lop that is unshowable because it has a lovely new coat on top with a tatty old coat down the sides and underneath.

You can assist the moult by clearing the loose hair, which is best done with what is often called a 'cat scrubber' (Mikki sell one under the trade name of 'Zoom Groom') but never use the scrubbers designed for dogs as they are too hard, although the cat one with its soft rubber protrusions has been found to be ideal on the lops' coat. If you work the scrubber from the front of the lop towards the back end with a gentle but firm hand you will find the amount of hair that is removed is quite amazing. Removing this dead, loose hair encourages the growth of new hair.

Grooming. Photos: Lea Fletcher

Once a lop is clear of moult then the majority of routine grooming is done with the hand, simply by smoothing and rolling the coat as you work from front to back. This will bring the coat into condition as the oils released from your hand will lubricate the hairs.

Some additional work may be required around the back end and underneath the lop and this is best done with a steel dog comb. Obviously extreme care is needed when using the comb around the genitals of a buck, but this is one area, particularly on an 'active' buck, that will need attention especially before showing.

Preparation of lops for showing is covered in detail in Chapter 6, but for routine maintenance a good diet supplemented by regular hand grooming and occasional combing underneath should be sufficient to keep the lop in good condition. The grooming of the two breeds of Cashmere lops is covered in Chapters 7 and 13.

A final but very important area that must be covered when discussing the maintenance of lops is vaccination against the two killer diseases Myxomatosis and Viral Haemorrhagic Disease (VHD).

The history of the Fancy is littered with the disaster stories of breeders who have chosen not to vaccinate against these two killers and suffered the consequence i.e. they lost much of their stock and in doing so lost many years of dedicated breeding.

There cannot be any excuse for not vaccinating against both these diseases. Both diseases are out there and will go through an entire stud like the proverbial 'dose of salts'.

Routine vaccination is the only way to guarantee your stock's immunity and it is as important as any other part of your maintenance routine.

It cannot be stressed enough that all rabbits are creatures of habit and therefore the lop owner must similarly become a creature of habit – it is only by establishing routines that anything outside the norm will be spotted and can quickly be treated, thus avoiding a potential disaster.

Chapter 5
Breeding Lops

*Marlene, the author's English Lop doe, with (above) her new-born babies
and (below) at one week old*

Whether you keep your lops for pet or show there can be no greater joy than seeing the doe give birth to a litter of tiny hairless, blind kits and then raising them through the various stages to be healthy young rabbits.

It is by no means a simple process, as any experienced rabbit breeder will tell you. The old saying 'breeding like rabbits' could not be further from the truth. The whole process from mating, through pregnancy and birth to the raising of the kits is analogous to the 110metre hurdler standing on the starting line looking down the line of hurdles and only just being able to see the finishing line in the distance; he may well fall at any one of the hurdles and therefore never reach the finish, but he can learn through experience, knowledge and skill to negotiate the hurdles and thus know as he stands at the start that if all goes well then he stands a very good chance of reaching that elusive finish line. So thus the potential breeder of lops must gain the experience, skill and knowledge to successfully breed and raise young lops.

However, before you commence any breeding programme you must assume that all will go well and that you will raise a healthy litter of young lops; you must therefore consider what you are going to do with the youngsters because you could well raise anything from two to maybe as many as ten or even twelve and it is highly unlikely that you will be able to keep them all.

If you are breeding pet rabbits then you may well be able to find a pet shop that will buy them from you. They will almost certainly will not give you very much for them, but it is well worth checking with your local pet shops that they will buy them from you before you mate your lops.

If you are breeding for showing then you have a lot of other considerations to take into account; many of the breeds of rabbits kept for showing are unsuitable for pets but this is one problem that breeders of lops do not have, as generally speaking the lops make first class pets.

However, extreme care must be taken in finding homes for the big lops (Meissner, French and English) as they really are not suitable for young children or even those adults with no experience of keeping rabbits.

In the unlikely event that all the offspring are of show standard then you must be able to choose the best to keep and find homes for the remainder; but of course you do not want to sell them locally where they could appear later on in competition against those you have kept. There will always be a market for good quality show lops but you may have to advertise further afield to find buyers. Whatever, you must make arrangements for the disposal of the surplus youngsters before you commence breeding.

If you intend to breed your lops purely for pets then the background, type and colour of the parents will not be so important as it is for the breeder of show quality animals. However, the health and vigour of the young rabbits is equally important whether they are for show or pet.

It is therefore absolutely imperative that only healthy stock, free from all inherited and genetic faults, are used for breeding. Perhaps the most common fault in a lot of breeds of rabbit, but particularly in lops, is the malocclusion of the teeth. This fault is an inherited trait and even if the offspring do not display it they may well carry it on to the next generation so therefore it is most important that you know the background of your breeding stock and that you do not breed from any stock that either displays malocclusion or has the fault in its background.

Having decided, to the best of your ability, that your potential breeding stock does not carry any inheritable faults then you must get them in the peak of condition. The mating itself is very stressful on the buck but this is nothing compared to the stress the birth and raising of a family of kits imposes on the doe.

If you intend to breed lops for showing then you do so to improve your stock; you always want to produce offspring that resembles the standard more closely than anything you presently own.

This is of course much easier said than done. It is the art of breeding; it is an art that generations of Fanciers have dedicated their lives to. Perhaps the most important requirement for the breeding of show quality stock is top quality parents that display some or all of the traits that you are trying to replicate – you cannot make a silk purse from a sow's ear – you cannot expect to produce top quality show lops from inferior parents.

A quick look at the Breed Standard (Chapters 7- 14) will show just how important 'Type' is for all the breeds of lop. Whilst it is acceptable for those who have exceptional type in their stock to breed for the improvement of finer detail, like colour or coat texture, the majority of breeders will spend many years breeding for type.

No matter how good the colour or condition is of a show lop it will never win at shows if it lacks type and every breeder must concentrate on breeding for and improving type.

Mendel's 'Laws of Inheritance' make it quite clear "like breeds like" therefore in theory this should be very simple; mate a very typey buck to a very typey doe and the offspring will be typey. However, even a rudimentary understanding of genetics will show why this is not always the case.

Even if you are not interested in reaching great heights on the show bench and only want to breed pet rabbits then you still want to breed from does that are good mothers and raise large healthy litters. Genetics is a vast topic and there are many good books that are dedicated solely to the subject, therefore here, the mechanism of inheritance, the objects of improvement, environment and inheritance and systems of breeding will be introduced using the minimum of scientific jargon, to hopefully whet the reader's appetite and encourage further study into these complex topics.

Whilst the final attributes of any rabbit may have been greatly affected by the environment in which it has been kept, all the characteristics it is born with are inherited from its parents; all being contained in an egg from the dam (mother) and a single sperm from the sire (father) that unites with this egg.

Both the sire's sperm and the dam's egg contain a miniscule body known as a nucleus and both these nuclei contain 22 sausage-like bodies known as chromosomes. In an individual the 22 chromosomes are in pairs, however the nuclei of the egg and sperm only contain one half of the chromosome pair so that when they unite in breeding the resultant nucleus contains its correct 22 pairs of chromosomes with one half of each being contributed from each parent. This is the basis of genetic inheritance, half of each parent's attributes being combined in a new body.

Each chromosome carries a large number of genes, it is these genes that carry the traits or characteristics that we see. As we can see from above, because each parent donates only one half of the chromosome pair, then similarly only one half of the gene pair comes from each parent. One of many complications to this basic principle is that some genes are dominant (denoted by a capital letter) whilst others are recessive (donated by a small letter). A pair of genes in any individual will be identical, but remember each parent donates one half of the offspring's gene pair. To understand this concept consider the following example:

The original Agouti rabbit contained a dominant gene 'A' (the distinctive agouti pattern) and over time this gene has mutated to 'a' (self). Remembering that 'A' is dominant and 'a' is recessive therefore what you see as an agouti may be an AA or Aa as they would look the same.

Suppose we now mate two agouti rabbits. In the first case we will assume that both the sire and the dam are AA and as the sire donates one gene and the dam the other it can be seen that the only possible outcome would be offspring that are AA.

If one parent was AA and the other Aa (remember this parent would still look like an agouti as A is dominant to a), then the resultant offspring could be AA or Aa, but would still look like agouti as both have the dominant A.

Now if both parents were Aa we have an entirely different situation as there are three possible outcomes AA (agouti), Aa (agouti) or aa (self). This can best be represented in a chart:

Sperm from Buck

		'A' gene	'a' gene
	'A' gene	New individual AA-pure agouti	New individual Aa-impure agouti
Egg from Doe			
	'a' gene	New individual Aa-impure agouti	New individual aa-pure self

Therefore it can be seen that from this Aa to Aa mating we have a 3-1 chance of offspring being Agouti (although only 1 in 4 will be pure agouti and 2 in 4 impure agouti) and a 1 in 4 chance that it will be a self.

Let us look at another example that should clarify the situation. If we mate one very long eared (English Lop) to another long eared one, the offspring should be long eared. But if we mate a long eared rabbit to a short eared one then the offspring will be of medium length. However, if one of these medium length rabbits is then mated to a long eared one (say its own father) then there will be the same situation as for the agouti example above, i.e. 3 to 1 will be long eared.

From what has been said above it can be seen that when breeding for colour then true-bred lines will always guarantee the colour of offspring. If you have bought in one of your breeding stock then you cannot be sure that it is true for colour and it will be up to you to select from successive generations to establish that trueness.

The selection of two animals for mating to give a desired result is still very much an art. Whilst a knowledge of the constituent genes in the parents will help determine some of the offspring's characteristics, the alteration, mutation, linkage and blending of genes means that the outcome of all features is almost impossible to predict. A breeder cannot select for one characteristic alone, he must base his decision on a number of points that he has available to him in his stud or bring in stock because it has a desirable trait that he wishes to introduce. Returning to the maxim - you cannot make a silk purse from a sow's ear - it is the concentration of good points and the elimination of undesirable ones that is the essence of livestock improvement.

Whilst there are a variety of breeding systems employed by rabbit breeders, no one is ideal for all purposes and the one a breeder chooses to use will depend on what he is trying to achieve.

Inbreeding is a mating system in which rabbits more closely related than the average are mated i.e. brother to sister or parent to offspring. Whilst this will certainly have the effect of fixing desired characteristics it will also fix any undesirable ones that are almost certainly lurking in there.

Line Breeding is a form of inbreeding, but far less intense and probably the system most used by breeders of exhibition rabbits. The object of line breeding is to keep the strain (or line) all related to an individual, usually a prize-winning buck.

Imagine rabbits A (the prize winning buck) and B are mated to produce C which is mated to A to produce D which is mated to A to produce E. Line breeding will therefore increase the purity of the stock in relation to the qualities of the original prize winning buck.

Like-to-like breeding means the mating of animals which are similar in appearance, but not necessarily, (or even usually), similar in genetic constitution. This form of breeding will not 'fix' characteristics but will maintain genetic variability. It is likely that one or two 'flyers' may be produced by this method from an otherwise stud of average quality.

Crossbreeding is the mating together of two distinct and pure, or relatively pure, breeds. The first generation produced from such a mating may well exceed their parents as recessive genes will be masked; however, subsequent generations will rapidly deteriorate as the recessive genes combine to influence the offspring.

Of course this is the method by which new breeds are developed; however, whilst the first generation may well be superb animals it will take another three or four generations before the poor traits can be eliminated in favour of the desired ones.

The final animal that you put on the show bench is the result of its inheritance that you engineered as the 'breeder', but also the environment in which you as the 'stockman' raised and now keep it. There are many factors that affect the environment in which you raise and keep the rabbit including; diet, housing, management, contact with disease and handling.

The rabbit breeder is fortunate in that most, if not all environmental factors are within his control. Two examples will suffice here to show that the best genetic determination can be detrimentally altered by environmental factors.

Firstly, a pure bred black rabbit is kept in a garden out in the full sun of summer. Result: ruined, as the coat will acquire a brown tinge and the rabbit will not be showable.

Secondly, a rabbit is bred for size. Two massive lops are mated from a pure line of big lops. The offspring should all be big, but if fed on a poor diet or invaded by some disease that checks their growth then the genetically determined size may never be achieved.

Having considered all of the above and decided on a suitable

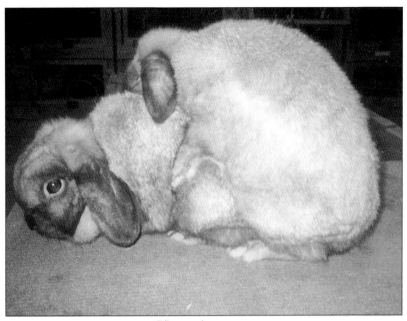

The mating process

pair of lops to breed from you must then check that the pair are in a suitable condition for mating. As was stated earlier they should both be in the peak of condition, no moult, neither over nor under weight, but fit. The buck should be checked to see that both his testes are descended, as it is quite normal for them to be withdrawn into the abdomen during moult. The doe should be checked for her readiness to mate; using your fore finger and thumb part the doe's vulva and if she is ready for mating it will be dark purple in colour. If it is pale pink she is not ready.

There are many ways of mating rabbits and most breeders have their favourite ways that they have used for years and found to work for them and therefore stick to. However an individual chooses to carry out the mating process it will almost certainly fit into one of the following three categories: put in a hutch together and left to get on with it; put on a bench together and allowed to get on with it with the minimum of interference but being watched for a successful coupling; or an assisted mating.

The large lops must be mated using the 'assisted' method, which is particularly important for English Lops where the weight of an amorous adult buck jumping onto the back of a doe can do irreparable damage.

By far the easiest method of mating rabbits is to put the doe in the buck's hutch (never put the buck in the doe's hutch, because she is territorial and will attack him).

They will usually circle around for a while and she may mount him if she is eager, also he may well try to mate her head. These are all normal functions of the rabbit's mating ritual and should not cause any concern.

If both are ready for mating then they will eventually sort things out. When she is ready you will see that she lifts her tail high up her back and once he has mounted her she will lift her back legs slightly; the two will then couple.

They stay coupled for a very short period of time; as the buck ejaculates he will grab the fur on her back with his teeth and at this time he will often let out quite a loud scream and then fall sideways off the doe; he falls because his feet are actually off the ground at the time of ejaculation.

If the two are in the buck's hutch they will usually retire to opposite corners and groom themselves. If left together they may mate again in an hour or so, but there is no need for the second mating at this time and it is quite in order to remove the doe back to her own hutch.

There are few things that can go wrong with this method of mating if you have checked both rabbits before putting them together and they are both ready for mating. If the doe just chases round and round the hutch and won't let the buck near her then clearly she is not ready and it is best to remove her and try again in a couple of days. A feisty doe that does not want to mate may well attack the buck and damage him, but this is unusual.

However, it is for this reason that most exhibitors do not use this method of mating. If you are trying to improve your stock then you could well be using your best show buck and you certainly cannot take the chance of him being injured.

Therefore a more controlled method of mating is to place both rabbits on a bench that has a non-slip surface (usually an old piece of carpet). You can then control the situation by holding the doe's head to prevent her either running away or turning on the buck.

This method also has the advantage that you are in a position to see that the mating definitely takes place. This may sound a bit superfluous as you might think that if you hear the buck let out his scream and see him fall over then a successful mating has taken place, but a young, inexperienced buck may well ejaculate prematurely when he has not even entered the doe.

The most common reason for the mating not taking place is the doe not lifting herself to the buck; in other words she just sits on it and prevents him entering her. Of course this does not happen with the assisted mating.

The assisted mating is not easy to carry out and the newcomer to large lops is advised to seek the assistance of an experienced large lop breeder to show them how to do it.

Basically with the doe on a bench (with a non slip surface) facing to your left put your left arm over the top of the doe so that you can put your left hand in her groin and use it to raise her back end at the appropriate time. Allow the buck to mount the doe and then get your right hand between the buck and the rear end of the doe so that you can get hold of her tail and pull it out of the way.

Extreme care should be taken when the buck ejaculates and you should be ready to let go of everything that you have been holding on to and grab the buck as he may well fall off the doe and hurt himself. Once you have mastered this method of mating lops you will find that it is in fact the best method of all as you know for certain when a successful mating has taken place.

An unwilling doe can be encourage to accept the buck by several methods, perhaps the most commonly used method is to remove the buck from his dirty hutch and put the doe in the hutch for a day or so. Although he is not present his scent is everywhere and this will usually get her in the mood.

It is also well known that the addition of a Vitamin E supplement to the doe's diet for a week or so prior to the mating can aid the doe's fertility. Vitamin E can be administered as Wheat germ Oil, as sunflower seeds or even toasted brown bread; however care must be taken not to overdo it as too much vitamin E can cause the blood to overheat, the result of which is that the doe will go into moult. This is the last thing you want her to do when she is pregnant.

If both the buck's testicles are descended it is very unusual for a buck not to want to mate a doe but sometimes a young buck will need placing on the doe's back just to give him the idea of what he is supposed to do. However, the reverse – an over zealous buck – is much more likely.

If a successful mating has been achieved then the doe should be returned to her hutch and left as quiet as possible. In order to ensure success many breeders will mate the doe again some ten to twelve hours later.

That, as they say, is all there is to it. The buck will continue his normal life whilst the doe should lead a relatively quiet life and under no circumstances should she be overfed. It is relatively unusual for the doe to show any signs of problems throughout the pregnancy; often a doe that has been quite nasty prior to mating will become placid and friendly. Occasionally a doe may chew the fur from her front feet and legs, quite why it is not known but it does not seem to adversely affect the outcome of the pregnancy.

The gestation period for rabbits is 30 – 32 days. It is unusual for them to give birth earlier than 30 days but is quite common for them to go over that time. However, whilst normal live babies can be born up to the 34th day, if the doe should go over 34 days then the babies are usually born dead. It is not uncommon for the doe to go 36 days in which case she will invariably give birth to one very large dead baby.

You will usually not notice anything different about the doe's behaviour during the early part of the pregnancy, but if she starts pulling hair from her chest and running around with mouthfuls of hay at about 18 days then she is almost certainly having a phantom pregnancy and should be re-mated without delay as she will be highly fertile at this time. Remember, if this does happen and you do re-mate, that the 30 day gestation period has started again.

If the doe starts nest building any time after about 21 days then there should be nothing to worry about. Some does seem to like to get their nest ready early whilst others leave everything till the last minute, in fact, some don't even make the nest until after they have given birth.

During the last week of the pregnancy the observant breeder will notice that the doe often lies with her legs stretched out behind her or even on her side. If you sit her on the bench and run your fingers along her chest and stomach you will feel her protruding nipples. It would be nice to say that you will see or feel the stomach swollen with the babies, and in some cases, especially with the big lops, you certainly can, but in many they really show very little outward signs of the litter they are carrying.

As the time of the birth arrives the doe's hutch should be thoroughly cleaned and disinfected; she should then have a generous layer of shavings and plenty of good quality barley straw. Most does will take large quantities of straw in their mouths and start nest building a day or so before they give birth and will start pulling hair from their chests to line the nest, but many, particularly first timers, do not conform to the norm.

There is little point sitting up all night with a doe the night she is due to give birth as for one thing she probably will not give birth the night you think she will but mainly because there really is very little you can do to help her.

There is much that can go wrong at the birth but your presence will more than likely just add additional stress to an already stressful situation. You should of course check the doe regularly to ensure all is well. What should happen is that you check her and find that she has cleaned up all the afterbirth and blood and is sat contentedly with her new-born family tucked up warmly in a lovely fur-lined nest. However this is not always the case, so let us look at some of the things that can and do go wrong.

Perhaps the most common problem is a 'scattered litter' which is where the new born kits are literally scattered around the hutch. They may be alive or they may not; often they are just alive with their tiny mouths and limbs just moving but they are cold.

If the doe has some kits in the nest and one or two scattered then it is often worth putting the cold scattered kit deep in the nest and allowing the warm kits to gradually raise the temperature of the cold kit. If the kit is not too chilled it may well make a full recovery.

If they are all scattered and there are no warm kits to help raise the temperature of the cold ones then the breeder's ingenuity is called for. Certainly it is not unknown for ladies to put the cold kits in their bra (the one they are wearing) as this certainly keeps them safe whilst they are slowly warming up.

Other methods include a box lined with rabbit fur in the airing cupboard – suspending them in warm water, with only their heads above the water – any method that slowly raises the body temperature may work. Do not be disappointed if none of these methods work as the chances of success are very low. But, as every breeder always says, you have to try everything you can.

Some does can be over zealous in their cleaning up of the new-born kits and afterbirth and in doing so can accidentally remove or partly remove either ears, limbs or tails. If she does do this but still puts them all in a good nest then you may well not be aware of the damage caused until the kits start coming out of the nest many days later.

If the damaged kits are scattered around the hutch and you find them it is usually best to put them down immediately as, with the exception of bits nipped out of ears or the end of a tail being bitten off, which the lop can happily live without, it really is not fair to let the rabbit live what will undoubtedly be a life of pain and misery. Unfortunately things can be worse; some does seem to have cannibalistic tendencies inbred into them. If any doe eats her own kits on more than one occasion she should be removed from the breeding programme as she may well be perpetuating the trait.

Some does, especially in the summer months, will not make a nest at all and just leave the kits in the shavings; plucking some hair from the doe's chest and building a nest around the kits can easily solve this problem. To pluck the hair from the doe simply take the doe from her hutch and turn her upside down in the crook of one of your arms and then with the fingers of the opposite hand gently pluck the hair in front of the front legs. You will find that it comes out quite easily and with a little patience you will soon amass sufficient to line a nest.

If the doe is in great distress following what should have been the birth then you must take immediate action, for it is not uncommon for the doe to get a kit stuck in the birth canal. You will recognise a doe that is in distress as she will be quite noisy, grunting and groaning and shuffling around the hutch.

Care should be taken when handling a doe in this condition as quite naturally she could well be quite aggressive and may attack you. However, you must get her out of the hutch and turn her over to check her. If you can see a kit half in and half out then you should try to remove it by gentle pulling.

If you cannot remove the kit then you must take the doe to the Vets immediately. If you act promptly then you will almost certainly save the doe and she will have absolutely no after effects. You will lose the kit but if there are others still in the womb then there is every chance that they will be born perfectly O.K. However, if you are slow to react to this situation there is a very good chance of losing the doe and kits.

A doe may have one or two dead kits in amongst an otherwise healthy litter and even if you think all has gone well and you can see pink, hairless kits squirming around in the nest you should remove the doe from the hutch and then part the fur with your finger tips. Gently poke around with your finger tip and check that all is well.

If a dead kit is found, remove it and cover the remaining kits up with the nest fur. When you return the doe to the hutch give her a titbit so that she is distracted for a while and does not go straight to the nest to see what you have been doing.

Once the immediate problems surrounding the birth are overcome you should feed the doe, giving her some additional greens as this will help with her fluid intake and consequentially her milk production. Try to leave her as peaceful as possible. This is not the time for the children and Uncle Tom Cobbly and All to be having a look, there is plenty of time for that later.

Many first-time breeders become concerned that the doe is not feeding her young. In the wild, rabbits only return to their nest of young once a day and then only stay for a very short while to feed the kits. New-born kits can survive the first 36 hours of their lives without being fed and so when the doe does feed them you may well not see her doing it.

In the wild the doe's natural instinct would be to flee the nest in order to attract a predator to her and not the nest, so whilst your lop may be confined in a hutch and cannot flee the litter when she hears you approaching she certainly can go to other side of the hutch and thus give you the impression that she never feeds them.

Only occasionally will a doe neglect to feed her young. You will not know if this is the case until beyond the thirty six hour point when the kits will be thin and will die within the next day or so.

Should a doe only have one kit then milk production can be a problem as does produce milk in response to the suckling of the young and one kit will not stimulate the glands sufficiently to produce milk.

This problem can be overcome by feeding the doe full-fat goats milk. Putting the milk in a water bottle on her hutch is the best way to do this, she will soon get the taste for it and it will not only strengthen her milk but also increase its quantity.

Full-fat goats milk is readily available from the major supermarkets in Britain and can be useful on young French and English lops even when the doe is producing milk normally. Both the French and English lop standards call for the adult specimen to be as large as possible and therefore it is desirable to get a youngster off to as good a start as possible.

Feeding the nursing doe full-fat goats milk will certainly get the kits off to a flying start and if the breeder continues to put the bottle of milk on the hutch once the youngsters start feeding themselves they will drink it and thus supplement the milk they are getting from their mother.

Once a doe has settled with her new family and is feeding the young then there is usually little that goes wrong until weaning time. The kits will start to fur up at about eight days old and their eyes will open at about twelve days and if they are being well fed by the mother they will remain in the nest until about the eighteenth day.

However, if the kits are hungry they will come out of the nest prior to the eighteen day point in search of food. They will usually make their own way back to the nest but should a kit be found out of the nest it should be put back in it immediately.

If for any reason the doe should die either at the time of the birth or shortly afterwards then the breeder is left with a litter of live kits and no doe to raise them.

There are two courses of action open to the breeder, either hand rearing the kits or, if another doe has kindled at the same time, fostering the kits. As fostering is by far the best course of action then it is prudent for the breeder to always mate at least two does at a time so that a foster mother is available should one be needed.

Fostering kits is relatively simple. Remove the doe that is to become the foster mother from its hutch and then rub the kit to be fostered in some of the dirty bedding in the foster mother's hutch. Place the kit deep in the nest, return the foster mother to her hutch and feed her a titbit to distract her from going straight to the nest. Some breeders will put a dab of Vick (nasal rub) on the doe's nose to temporarily dull her sense of smell. It is highly unusual for a doe to reject a fostered kit.

If you are forced to hand raise the kits then you should commence it knowing that you are highly unlikely to succeed. Certainly there are those that do raise one or two kits this way but it is not easy.

When the youngsters are very small it is probably best to keep them in a box lined with nesting material in the house where you can keep them warm. You will require a kitten bottle-feeding kit that comes complete with teats and a small feeding bottle. The secret of success lies in 'little and often' and what you use to feed the kits on is very much open to debate; Lactol, Kitten Milk or Goats Milk all have their devotees and for every breeder you find that has had success with one of them you can find one that will say "that does not work".

In other words, there are no hard and fast rules about what to use and not use. Like so many things with rabbits you use what works for you and the same can be said for quantities. Many books have charts laying down the quantities that kits should drink at specific ages. However, the best guideline is that you fill them up, but don't overfill them. A bit like getting the wind out of a baby, you will have to stimulate the kit to urinate for the first few days of its life and to do this you must rub the area around the genitals until the kit urinates.

If you have embarked on hand rearing you will have to keep it up at the same level until the kits are about three weeks when they

will start eating solids.
Even when they do
start on solids the
bottle-feeding should
continue for another
two weeks or so,
obviously decreasing
the quantity as time
goes by.

Although kits will
normally come out of
the nest at about three
weeks of age extreme
care should be taken

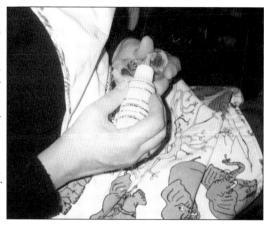

when the door to the hutch is open or they are picked up, as they
really have very little control of their movements and are highly
likely to 'bounce' straight out of your hand. This is certainly not a
time for children to handle the kits. Within a week or so, i.e. at
about four weeks of age, the kits will have far greater control of
their movements and although you should still be very careful how
they are handled they are quite manageable.

With the exception of the English Lops, all lop kits look like
miniature versions of the adult at about four weeks of age. This is
obviously a good time to look carefully and critically at your litter;
check their sex, check their teeth, check all the feet have all the toes,
then position the youngster so that you can have a really good look
at its type.

To the first-time breeder this may seem a strange thing to do to a
four week old lop but from about five weeks until about fourteen
weeks they go through a period of maximum bone growth and tend
to get long and straggly. This makes them very hard to assess at the
time you are likely to be selling your surplus stock. It is therefore
best to make the big critical decision at four weeks and decide who
is staying and who will be going, unless you are in the fortunate
position of being able to keep all the litter until they are about four
months old. By then you will have a very good idea just how good
each individual is likely to become at maturity.

A litter that has been born and raised with no problems will require no special feeding. From the day that the litter was born the doe's food ration should be increased. Certainly for the smaller lops the amount of food should be doubled; if the doe had been fed once a day, say evenings, then you would feed the same quantity at the evening feed and again in the morning. For the larger lops that are already being fed twice a day then a fifty percent increase in the amount fed will suffice until the kits are running around.

English Lop doe and kits

All lops' kits will start eating from their mother's bowl at about three weeks of age, at first this will supplement the doe's milk. The doe's milk will start to dry up once the kits are about four weeks old; however, the weaning process must be slow and if they are given the chance many young kits will continue to suckle their mothers up until about twelve weeks of age.

Kits should certainly never be removed from their mother before they are six weeks of age; if you can leave them with the mother for longer then it is to their advantage. There really is only one reason to remove the mother from her babies and that is if she (the doe) is abusing them (the kits). Does will often try to mount the kits and can make their lives a misery and should this happen then they will have to be separated.

Always remove the doe to a new hutch leaving the kits in the hutch they have been raised in. The kits should then remain together as a family unit for as long as they remain on good terms. You may find that at about twelve weeks of age the bucks in the litter, rather like teenage boys, will start fighting and may well start to mount any does in the litter. This in itself is not a problem as bucks do not become fertile until about sixteen weeks of age, it is however the disturbance to the family harmony that causes the problem.

Obviously if you intend to sell any of the litter they should be removed from their siblings and kept on their own for an absolute minimum of a week before you allow them to leave your shed.

If you intend to keep any of the litter for showing then they must have British Rabbit Council rings fitted: there is no precise age at which rings should be fitted as you will find that you can easily fit an 'H' ring to an English Lop up to about twelve weeks of age, whereas the French Lop would have to have its 'H' ring fitted at between eight and ten weeks of age and a mini lop would need its 'K' ring fitting at about six weeks of age. Only experience will tell you the right age. If you put them on too early the worst that can happen is that they fall off, if you leave it too late you can never show that lop.

It may seem reading this chapter that the breeding of lops is fraught with problems, and there certainly are plenty of obstacles to overcome but there can be no greater joy than seeing a lop that you have bred sat on that top table receiving Best in Show.

Chapter 6
Showing Lops

*Above: pair of English Lops bred by the author with (centre) the
National English Lop Club's silver cup, first awarded in 1900.*

*Below, Agouti Dwarf Lop exhibited by Kevin Wakefield,
best in show at the Jubilee Championship Show held in Sheffield in 2002*

Steward at a Lop show

LOPS have been shown for as long as there have been rabbit shows; the English Lop is rightly known as the King of the Fancy because it was the first rabbit to be bred purely for showing and for no other reason. Whilst all the other breeds of lop have been 'created' or imported into Britain in the last fifty years or so, the English Lop has been shown for over two hundred years and in fact the beautiful silver trophy awarded to the winner of the English Lop Adult Stock Show each year dates back to 1900.

The British Rabbit Council as we know it today did not come into existence until 1934 but 'The Lop' (as the English Lop was then called) had been extremely popular long before then with huge sums of money often on offer for the biggest or longest eared lop and even larger sums being wagered around the table.

If we ask the question 'Why Show Lops' then we must also ask 'Why Show Rabbits at all', as the lops only account for eight of the fifty plus breeds of rabbit that are exhibited today. If we are now asking why people exhibit rabbits then similarly we have to ask why anyone exhibits any animal or bird.

The stock answer must always be to 'improve the breed' but of course the majority of those exhibiting any animal or bird are just trying to get their stock to be as good as that of those who are winning and it really is only those very few top winners with many years of experience that are actually pushing the breed forward and 'improving the standards'.

Show rabbits, just like show dogs and cats, are judged against an artificial standard that has been agreed by those who are showing at that point in history; therefore the requirements of any breed are continually evolving. The British Rabbit Council publishes a new breed standard every five years and it is during the intervening five years that the various Breed Clubs (who own the Breed Standard for each breed) will try to come to agreement, usually through AGM's, on changes that they wish to see implemented.

So having accepted that the majority of us breed and show our rabbits against a purely artificial standard, why do we do it?

Many fanciers will tell you that they go to shows to have a day out with their friends and that they really do not care whether their rabbits win or lose. It is certainly true that the rabbit fancy is like a great big family and those that are in the Fancy have a common bond – rabbits – but there is much more to it than that. Life-long friends are made in the Fancy, the kind of friends who will come to

Transferring Lops from their travelling box to the show pens

your assistance when you are in need; the kind you know you can rely on for help.

So it is no wonder that many exhibitors who do not aspire to win at shows, continue to go to shows week in and week out just to be with their friends. With about a thousand shows a year throughout Britain and the considerable costs involved in motoring these days there must be something more than just friendship that motivates Fanciers.

Of course we all love our lops, we would not put so much time and effort in to keeping them if we did not, so surely it must be the competitive streak in most of us that drives us to get out of bed before dawn on a freezing winter's morning, drive half way across the country to spend all day in a draughty village hall and then drive home in the dark, all on our day off from work.

Whilst many Fanciers would still insist that they are not competitive in nature there is no greater joy than seeing a rabbit that you have bred, raised and got into perfect condition winning honours at a show. You only have to see the smiles on the faces of the children at shows as they collect their prizes for their winning pet rabbits and the disappointment on the faces of those that have not won (in fairness most shows make sure that all the children go home with something) to realise that the competitive spirit is a part of our nature.

In order to just exhibit at rabbit shows some knowledge and experience of what is happening is required; in order to compete at rabbit shows you must add patience, a thick skin and the art of listening and learning to knowledge and experience. Those that win regularly at shows have been dedicated to the art of breeding and exhibiting for many years and anyone taking up this wonderful hobby must accept at the outset that success is unlikely to come quickly and without numerous setbacks and a few heartaches.

Before you can exhibit you have to acquire 'show quality' stock. This is often not easy as you are unlikely to find show quality rabbits for sale in a Pet Shop, and you must therefore get in touch with established breeders. It is perhaps best to visit a few shows before you buy, in this way you can decide which breed and even which colours take your fancy.

It is easy to say that the newcomer should start with the easiest colour i.e. the Red Eyed White (REW) (whites are always white and two whites mated together will always breed whites) but of course they are not to everyone's liking; similarly, it would be easy to say that the newcomer should not start on the big lops if they are not used to handling rabbits.

At the end of the day you will choose the colour and breed that appeals to you most. However, if you can visit a few shows and talk to the breeders who are exhibiting you will get a better idea of what is available and be better able to decide not only what you like but also what you are capable of looking after.

Having decided which breed and what colours you like then you have to find a breeder who has some of them for sale. No breeder is ever going to sell his best rabbits, that is after all what he has been breeding for, to produce 'the winner' – you must therefore accept that whilst you may be able to buy some very good rabbits they may not be show winners.

A lot of breeders will part with an older buck that may well have been a big winner when it was young, and is now suitable only for stud. If you can get that breeder to part with a pair of does from the same line then you have what we call a 'trio' and have the basis with which to breed your own stock.

Whilst you may be able to buy lops that are ready for showing the real pleasure comes when you breed your own winners. Therefore the trio is the ideal unit to buy to get going. This is not always possible and sometimes you have to put a buck from one stud with a doe from another – this may or may not work. However you get the foundation stock to start your stud there is no substitute for the most important ingredient – patience.

Before you can enter a rabbit show you must be a member of the British Rabbit Council, the BRC. There are a variety of memberships available to suit individuals: Junior, Adult, Stud/ Partnership, Family and even ones for Students and Pensioners. You can join through their website, over the phone or by writing. On becoming a member you will receive a variety of information packs including the breed standards book, these will really get you going. The BRC is also there to help its members and the staff at the

Headquarters at
Newark is always
available to
a n s w e r
questions; you
do not have to
worry how stupid
your question
may seem, they
have heard them
all before and
their friendly
advice may just
prevent the
newcomer making a costly error.

Mrs J Duffy's Dwarf Lop, best in show at a recent Southern
Championship Show

As well as becoming a member of the BRC most Fanciers
subscribe to the 'Fur & Feather', a monthly magazine that contains
the magazine 'RABBITS' with all the show results and advertisements
for forthcoming shows, as well as numerous articles and photographs
of interest to breeders and exhibiters of all small animals. Like joining
the BRC you can subscribe to Fur & Feather on their web site, over
the phone or by writing to them.

All rabbits that are exhibited at BRC supported shows in Britain
must wear a BRC ring on one of their hind legs. Once you are a
member of the BRC you can buy these rings to put on any rabbits
you breed. Each breed of rabbit recognised by the BRC has been
allocated a ring size that is denoted by a letter (see the breed chapters
Ch 7 – 13 for each breed's ring size).

The ring has the letters BRC followed by the year (04 for 2004)
and then the letter denoting the size of the ring. Therefore the breed
of the rabbit (a Miniature Lop has a K ring, whereas a Dwarf Lop
has a C ring). This is followed by a unique number that is registered
to the breeder. Thus a ring could well have a number like
BRC04K01234. This ring will be registered to the breeder who
bought the rings from the BRC and will identify that rabbit
throughout its life.

If you are a newcomer and buying lops that someone else has

bred then the breeder will have put rings on them that are registered in their name. You must then get the breeder to give you a signed transfer card to complete and send with the appropriate fee to the BRC so that their records can be amended and you can be recorded as the new owner. Once you have transferred any lops you have purchased to your name you can enter them in BRC supported shows.

To find out where and when shows are being held and just as importantly when and to whom entries must be submitted, you should subscribe to the magazine 'RABBITS' that is issued monthly with 'Fur and Feather'. Every BRC supported show must be advertised in RABBITS so if you have the magazine then you can be sure that you know about every show that is taking place.

The major Championship shows and some of the Agricultural shows that are held during the summer months usually require entries to be sent by post, often weeks in advance. However, the Show Secretary usually takes entries for most 'normal' village hall shows over the phone during the week prior to the show. You should study the show advertisement in 'RABBITS' and decide which classes your rabbits can be entered in.

If you are a newcomer and are unsure of all the abbreviations used in the advertisement explain this to the Secretary when you phone and they will always help you to get it right. For one thing, they want you to enjoy your visit to their show so that you come back again; every fancier was a newcomer at some time and most can still remember how glad they were of help when they started.

The majority of shows these days advertise 'block entry' which means that you pay one fee that covers all the classes that your lop could possibly be judged in if it keeps winning through each round of judging. The majority of shows are judged as 'adult' and 'under five', this means that the judge first judges all the adults in a class (these will be those of the same breed and colour) and places them in order of merit. In Britain we judge using the comparative judging system, where the judge 'compares' all the rabbits in front of him against the breed standard and the one that most closely resembles the standard is the winner.

When the judge has decided his order of merit of the adults in a class, all except the winner are sent back to their pens. The winning rabbit remains on the table and the judge reads out the rabbit's ring number that the book steward records on the judging sheets. The judge then writes his comments on the winning adult rabbit and it is held at one end of the table by one of the stewards whilst he judges the under five month old rabbits in the same breed and class.

Using the same comparative system he selects his best u/5 and places the rest of the rabbits in the class in order of merit. All except the winning u/5 are then returned to their pens. The judge reads out the winning u/5's ring number for the book steward and writes his notes on the rabbit.

He now has two rabbits on the table, the winning adult and the winning u/5. Still using the comparative judging system he now judges the two rabbits and decides which most closely resembles the breed standard. The winner of these two rabbits is awarded the Challenge Certificate (CC). This CC is awarded by the BRC and counts towards making the rabbit a Champion. Great care should be taken with all CCs, as they will not be replaced by the BRC if lost.

These two winning rabbits are then returned to their pens and the judge continues with the next class, continuing judging all the colour classes within a breed. When he has judged all the classes in a breed, say the Dwarf Lops, he will, usually, bring all the CC winners back to the table and judge them to find the Best of Breed.

The term 'usually' was used deliberately as it is the judge's prerogative which rabbits he wants to see for the Best of Breed, as he may know from his class judging that a particular colour rabbit, although winning its CC, is not going to compete with the other CC winners and therefore decides that he does not want to see it again.

The Stewards and the Book Steward were mentioned in the last paragraph and need some explanation here: the Stewards may look very official in their white coats, usually adorned with badges, but they are in fact just ordinary Fanciers who are helping with the day's proceedings by getting the rabbits from their pens, looking after them on the judging table and then returning them safely to their pens when the Judge has finished judging them.

For the newcomer to exhibiting, stewarding is the best place to

Judging in progress on four tables at a regional championship show

learn about rabbits. The judge will usually make some comments as he is judging; but also the stewards handle all the rabbits that are being judged and therefore handle the best rabbits in the show and not only see, but feel, what makes a winning rabbit. So the sooner a newcomer gets themselves a white coat and joins in with the stewarding the quicker they will start learning.

Stewards must be aware of the standard of behaviour that is expected of them; of course the primary concern of any steward must be the safety of the rabbits in their care.

This responsibility starts from getting the rabbit from the pen and continues until the rabbit is safely shut back in its pen. The Stewards need to concentrate on the rabbits they are looking after and whilst they may be making conversation with the other stewards this should not detract from what they are there to do. As a Steward you will be required to get all breeds from their pens and whilst none of the Lop breeds is notoriously vicious or awkward, other breeds can be. Care must be taken with all breeds not to catch feet or legs on the pen doors and door frames and extra care is needed with the large lops that their backs are not scraped on the top of the door frame.

The Steward must not identify to the judge the owner of the rabbit they are stewarding, this also means that they must not point out its good or bad points; it is the Judge's job to find the good and bad in a rabbit. A Steward should treat all rabbits they steward equally; they should try to settle the rabbit on the table and position it in the accepted pose for the breed. Obviously this means knowing the pose for each breed but this will quickly be learnt by those who steward regularly and other experienced stewards will always help the inexperienced ones.

Some Judges like a lot of chat and banter at the table, seeing it as part of making a pleasant and enjoyable day; others will work in silence ignoring all that is going on around them. Any Judge will soon let the Stewards know what conduct they like at their table. Many fanciers like to steward their own rabbits; if you stand stewarding all day you will become aware of other fanciers who appear at the table whilst a particular breed is being judged and then disappear again, often to be replaced with another group whilst another breed is being judged.

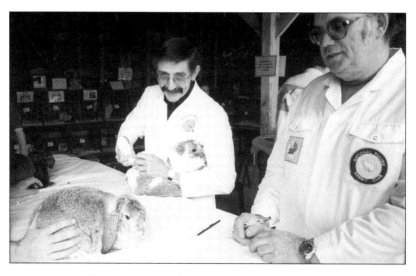

The author judging a Lop class. On his left is the Book Steward

Whilst, in theory, there is nothing wrong with stewarding your own rabbit, you must still adhere to the normal code of behaviour. 'Jockeying' is the stewarding of your own rabbit so as to either gain the judge's attention or so as to gain some sort of unfair advantage.

Whilst jockeying is not illegal it most certainly is frowned upon. In some ways it is understandable – if you have spent many hours training your rabbit to sit correctly on the table and show itself off then the last thing you want is to see is it badly handled by an inexperienced Steward.

Most judges will spot jockeying straight away and either take absolutely no notice of it, or take action to counter it.

Stewarding is a pleasant way of spending a day at any show, it is where you will learn about all the breeds and pick up snippets of information that will all add to your general understanding of rabbits.

The Book Steward stands on the same side of the table as the Judge. It would be wrong to call him the Judge's Assistant, for a good Book Steward can keep the day going and get everything finished up with the least inconvenience to all, whereas, a disorganised or inexperienced Book Steward can spoil the whole day.

Taking on the role of Book Stewarding is not to be done lightly as it involves standing on one's feet for the whole day and applying a high level of concentration and organisation. Once a Fancier has a good understanding of showing and the show rules then they can volunteer to be a Book Steward; however, it is best to learn at small shows that have low numbers of rabbits and plenty of time to judge them in, and even then, to have an experienced Book Steward show them the ropes.

Both stewarding and book stewarding are requirements for those who aspire to be Judges, but more importantly both are roles in which the Fancier learns an enormous amount about rabbits and showing them.

To return to the show and judging of rabbits; the rabbits exhibited at a show are divided into four sections: Lops, Fancy, Fur and Rex, although these sections may be combined into Lops/Fancy and Fur/Rex at smaller shows and depending on the popularity of each breed in the area the show is being held.

We are obviously concerned here with the Lop Section. It was formally recognised by the BRC in 2000 (previously Lops were part of the Fancy section). Hence when the Judge judging the Lops has completed all the breed classes 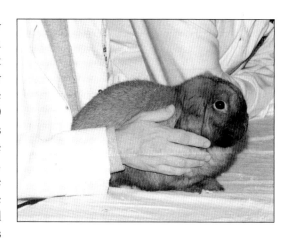 he will then judge to find his Best Lop.

This may be done in several ways and is entirely at the Judge's discretion. He may simply bring out all his Best of Breeds and place them in order; or he may bring out all his best adults and place them and then bring out all the under five month winners and place them in order. Having done that he will put the two together.

This can result in what can at first sight appear to give some odd decisions; but as long as there is no 'cross-judging' (putting a rabbit in front of another that has already beaten it in a previous class) then there is no problem. It could be that a Judge feels that his best three lops are all under five month lops and that they are all say, Miniature Lops; as long as none of the under fives was beaten by adults in their class and the under five that the Judge makes his Best Lop was Best of Breed Mini Lop then this is not a problem. It is when judging gets as complicated as this that a good book steward is worth his or her weight in gold.

The winner of the Best Lop Diploma also wins an additional 'star' towards any future championship claim. All BRC supported shows have a star ranking from One to Five (although there was a special one-off six star show at Stafford in 2000).

As a rough guide one star shows are usually put on for Trainee Judges to learn their craft, two star shows are the normal shows held in village halls throughout the country every week, three star shows are either breed stock shows or specials such as Agricultural shows, four star shows are championship shows and there are only two five star shows a year – London and Bradford.

This is only a rough guide as there are often exceptions. However, the Judge at a show will award CC's with a star value equivalent to the star ranking support given by the BRC. Thus two star CC's are awarded at a two star show. However, the Lop Diploma winner will be able to count the diploma as an extra star so that a Lop Diploma awarded at a four star show is worth five stars.

Once a Judge has finished judging his section he must get together with the judge or judges of the other sections in the show so that they can jointly decide their Best in Show.

Let us imagine a normal two star village hall show that has one Judge judging Lops and Fancy and another judging Fur and Rex (this is by far the most common situation).

Our Lop judge will have to judge the Fancy rabbits as well as his lops; on completion of both Sections he will have his Best Lop and his Best Fancy. Similarly the Fur and Rex Judge will on completion of his judging produce his two section winners; Best Fur and Best Rex.

The two Judges now get together and decide the order the four rabbits go in, with the winner being awarded Best in Show. Like the Lop Diploma judging described above this Best in Show judging can be just as complicated. The judge may decide not to bring one of his diploma winners to the BiS table or he may decide to bring two Lops and no Fancy. The permutations are endless but as long as no cross-judging takes place and the judges find their best rabbit then all is well and above board.

The newcomer to a show may well have watched their rabbit being judged and seen the judge record its ring number and then heard him say that the rabbit is awarded the CC, but then wonder why some time later no certificate has been put on the rabbit's pen. This is because the busiest person at any show is the Show Secretary and it may well take some time for the Secretary to catch up with the results and write out all the cards. If by the end of the show you have not received a 'card' that you think you should have then by all means ask the Secretary, but do not pester earlier, as it will almost certainly be on its way.

Shortly after the Best in Show judging is completed the club Treasurer will pay out prize money. You should collect all the cards from your rabbits' pen and take them to the treasurer who will calculate how much you have won. If you do not, either deliberately or by accident, collect your prize money then it will be assumed that you have donated it to the host Club. When Judging is completed you can 'lift' your rabbits and go home. It is a rule of all shows that no rabbits can be lifted until judging is completed so even if your rabbit was first to be judged in the morning and it did not win it must still stay in its pen until all judging is completed.

Now that the structure of the show has been discussed it is time to consider what you must do to not only prepare your lops for showing but to hopefully win at them. In Chapter Two, acquiring your lops was discussed in detail and it became apparent that to get started you would be buying from a recognised breeder and probably buying a trio so that you could breed your own show stock.

Unlike many other breeds of show rabbit, type is all important in all breeds of lop. It is absolutely essential that you have good type lops otherwise you will never win. As it can be quite difficult to interpret the written standard and visualise what the required 'type' is, it is advisable to visit shows and study the winners.

If you can, it is best to go to one of the major Championship Shows, preferably the London (late summer) or the Bradford (January). If you can go to either of these shows on the second day when all the prize cards are on the pens, then you can study those that have won cards and try and see the difference between those that won and those that did not win.

Obviously you cannot touch the exhibits and therefore you cannot feel what the Judge felt, as a very typy lop may not have been 'in coat' which may account for why a very good type rabbit did not win a card. However, you can guarantee that the winning lops will all be of very good type.

If you look closely you will notice the shortness of body and the extremely broad heads and see just how different these lops are to the pet shop lops. This is the type you must aspire to breed into your lops but unfortunately it does not come by accident and despite what you may hear about 'fliers' appearing in litters it is extremely unlikely that you will produce this kind of type in your lops unless you have it in your breeding stock.

If you get chatting to the breeders at the Championship Shows then they may well let you handle one of their lops. If you are lucky enough to get your hands on any of these top quality lops then hopefully you can fix that 'feel' in your mind so that you know just what you are aiming for in your breeding. If not, then it is the look of them that you will have to be content with.

Just as type is essential in a winning lop then so is 'condition'. A lop should be fit. By fit we mean that the lop should be well muscled and firm; this can only be achieved by the correct life-long maintenance regime being employed back home in the shed. Your lops must be fed correctly on quality food, they must be housed in sufficiently large hutches to allow them to exercise correctly and they must be completely free of moult.

Unfortunately we have very little control over when and for how long a rabbit moults and it may well be that you have bred a superb animal for a particular show and it goes into moult the week before the show. Your lop may well have very good type and then you may get away with a certain degree of moult at a small local show where there are small classes but at major championship shows there will always be someone with their lops in perfect condition and therefore, those that show any degree of moult are highly unlikely to get in the frame and are thus best left at home to prepare for another day.

So you have bred exceptional type into your lops and you have got them into very good condition, so now you must make sure that they are spotlessly clean. It is an insult to the Judge to put a dirty rabbit on the table for him to judge. The easiest way to prevent having to do an awful lot of work and spend a lot of time cleaning your lops for a show is not to let them get dirty in the first place.

Show rabbits should never be allowed to exercise on grass; they will stain their feet green and grass stain is one stain that is virtually impossible to remove. Similarly, they should never be kept on newspaper, as the ink will stain the feet – black ink stain, like grass stain. is equally difficult to remove. Show rabbits are best kept in hutches that can then be kept clean; this prevents them ever really getting dirty and makes show preparation a lot easier.

Even the cleanest lop will require some grooming and preparation for showing and this should be done well in advance of the show.

All lops' coats should 'roll'. This means that if you run an open hand through the lop's coat from its rear end towards its head then the coat should roll back into place, which is very different from some breeds of rabbits, like the Polish, that should have a 'fly back' coat.

It is the combination of guard hairs and the softer under coat that give a lop its rollback coat; the guard hairs are longer and sharper than the soft, denser undercoat.

The presence of guard hairs is an inherited trait and any lop that lacks guard hairs and has a very soft coat that will never roll back should not be used in a breeding programme.

You will often notice a Judge get his head down level with the lop he is judging and then take some of the fur on the lop's back between his thumb and forefinger; this is when he is looking for the presence of guard hairs.

A study of the Breed Standards (Chap 7-14) will show the importance put on the presence of guard hairs in all of the lops (except the English and Meissners that do not mention them).

The long hairs on the Cashmere and Miniature Cashmere lops are in fact guard hairs and their Standard gives 30 points for their presence.

The Dwarf Lop Standard puts so much emphasis on the presence of guard hairs that 10 points are given and the standard says that there should be an 'abundance of guard hairs' whereas the French, German and Miniature lops' Breed Standards all call for an 'abundance of guard hairs' but do not specifically allocate any points to their presence.

A lop's coat will only roll when it has the required proportion of guard hairs and is free of moult and dirt – by dirt we mean dust particles that any rabbit will pick up in its hutch. Whilst rabbits are meticulously clean animals that are constantly grooming themselves they still need a bit of time spending on them to ensure that their coats are really clean and free of dead hairs.

To clean a lop's coat you should rub a small amount of distilled witch hazel (available from any Chemist shop) into both of your hands so as to just make them both damp and then work your hands backwards and forwards through the lop's coat. This is best done about five days before the show. On each of the remaining days before the show you should 'dry groom' the lop. Dry grooming is simply done by sitting the lop on a grooming table and working your dry hands backwards and forwards through the coat. A combination of the oils in your skin and the oils released from the fur by the massaging will lubricate the coat and not only clean it but give it a beautiful healthy looking sheen. This method of grooming is essential if a quality lop is to stand any chance on the show bench and it cannot be carried out at the last minute.

Whilst wet grooming followed by a few days of dry grooming will get the top side of a lop in good condition a different approach is required for the underneath of the lop. Before you can groom the underneath of a lop you must learn to turn them over and keep them calm and controlled whilst you groom; with the small lops this is usually just a matter of lots of handling and then some more handling. Once the small lops become used to being turned over they will usually give you very few problems, however, the bigger lops are a different story altogether but once a very simple technique is learnt then your troubles will be greatly reduced.

To turn a large lop over onto its back, stand in front of a grooming table that has a non-slip surface, with the lop held against your chest. Support the lop with one hand holding the base of its ears and the other around the rump. The secret is that rabbits cannot kick if their spines are straight, so lower the rump of the lop onto the edge of the table and put the forefinger of the hand that is supporting the rump out straight so that it is along the spine, then allow that forefinger to apply a gentle pressure on the spine so that you can feel the spine straightening. Lower the head of the lop slowly down on to the table using your grip on the base of the ears to control the lowering action.

Once this method is perfected you will find that throughout the action the spine remains straight because the table surface gradually takes over the pressure from your finger to maintain that straightness of the spine. The lop will then be lying on its back with the firm surface of the table maintaining that all important straightness of the spine. The hand that supported the lop around the base of the ears should maintain its control whilst with the other hand that is now free can be used to gently but firmly stroke down the chest and belly, keeping the stroke going right through and over the back legs so that they extend and straighten out behind the lop.

The lop should now be lying calmly on its back on the table; until you have practised this many times and got the lop used to it you should not let go of the lop and start grooming but rather get someone else to do the grooming whilst the controlling hand keeps a firm hold.

The safest way to get the lop from this position back on to its feet is to allow it to roll over side ways and let go of the controlling hand that has been holding the base of the ears as the lop rolls, thus allowing it to naturally come back on to its feet.

Having mastered the turning over of your lop you can carry out the grooming to prepare it for showing.

The first thing that should be done is to trim the nails; this is not a difficult procedure and it is one that every lop owner must learn as it is a routine task for every rabbit, either show or pet. Even on dark coloured nails you can see the quick if you look carefully. The nails should be trimmed, using clippers designed for trimming the nails of small dogs, to within about a quarter of an inch of the quick; do not forget the dew claws on the inside of the front legs.

If you watch your lops in their hutches you will see that they use the inside of their front legs to wash their faces; therefore the first thing to check on the underneath of the lop is the inside of the front legs; if there is any matting whatsoever it should be combed out with a fine toothed comb.

Whilst checking the inside of the front legs it is worth checking the armpits because almost certainly the judge will. For some reason the smaller lops do not seem to suffer from matting in the armpits, however the larger ones do. Naturally the big lops do not like having their armpits combed out, especially if they have knots in them, as it hurts, therefore you will almost certainly need an assistant to help.

Having thoroughly checked the inside of the front legs you should comb the bib or chest in front of the front legs. A medium tooth steel comb is best for this and should only ever be used in the direction of the coat. Bucks have a scent gland under the chin and most adult bucks rub this gland on the woodwork in their hutch to mark it with their scent; you should particularly check this area on adult bucks as some can rub the gland so much that the area either becomes matted or in the worse cases bald.

If the lop is free of moult then there is likely to be little grooming required through the chest and stomach, however the back of the hind legs and the genital area will almost certainly require combing; obviously extreme care should be taken when working in this area.

Perhaps the most poorly prepared area of lops presented for showing is their feet; a lop with dirty feet is never going to win. Every experienced exhibitor has their own 'secret' way of cleaning a lop's feet, but all would agree that the real secret of success is not to let them get dirty in the first place.

Unfortunately this can be easier said than done with some rabbits that seem to be able to get themselves dirty in even the cleanest of hutches. The first two rules of cleaning feet is that you must not damage the fur colour and that you must not use artificial colourings of any kind (this is strictly against BRC rules and a rabbit will be disqualified if a Judge suspects the use of any artificial colourings).

I stated earlier that rabbits are fastidious in their cleaning, this natural process can be encouraged by mixing a paste of lemon juice and starch and spreading it on the feet with an old toothbrush. These are purely natural products and their application will cause the rabbit to lick its feet until it is removed, in doing so they will clean their feet. Similarly other concoctions can be used to encourage this process.

Perhaps the most common preparation used is 5% solution hydrogen peroxide (a mouth wash sold in all chemists) mixed with chalk powder to make a paste that is then applied to the feet. The rabbit will lick off the paste but because the 5% hydrogen peroxide is a very mild bleach solution it will whiten dirty white fur. Under no circumstances whatsoever should 5% hydrogen peroxide be used on any coloured fur as the bleaching effect will be to turn the coloured fur yellow.

On rabbits with coloured feet the 5% hydrogen peroxide solution can be replaced with distilled Witch Hazel as this has no effect on colour. A less radical method of cleaning feet is to use Vanish soap; however, care must be taken not to use too much water when washing off the soap as water could ruin a well-prepared coat.

Whatever method is used it is imperative that the lop's feet are spotlessly clean when it arrives on the show table for judging and that they are dry and free of any substance that you may have used to get them in that condition.

The rule of not using artificial colourings on the exhibition rabbit applies to the whole of the rabbit and not just to the feet, therefore any white hairs that are in an otherwise coloured coat must be removed rather than being dyed or coloured in any way. Of course if any coloured lop has more than 'a few' white hairs then perhaps it is not suitable as a show rabbit. A few white hairs can be removed with the very careful use of a pair of tweezers; to find white hairs in a coloured coat it is best to look at the rabbit from behind.

You may sometimes notice a Judge do this when examining an exhibit – turn it around and study it from behind – this is when he is looking for those stray white hairs that you have missed.

The only way not to miss any white hairs is for you to also look from behind under a very strong or natural light. Should you show Sooty Fawn lops then it is a fault for it to have a light tail and a disqualification if it has a white tail; neither of these tails are able to be altered in anyway and therefore you should discard a white tailed sooty and only show a light tailed one if you are prepared to be beaten or totally disregarded by some judges.

Similarly the butterfly pattern is very clearly defined and any deviation from the required pattern will lead to disqualification; you cannot use any artificial means to make it conform and therefore it is best discarded from your show team.

With the exception of the English Lop all the other lops should just have the inside of their ears checked for cleanliness; they will almost certainly be clean. However because the English Lop has such big ears and because so much emphasis is put on them when they are being judged they must be cleaned regularly.

Like the cleaning of a lop's feet all the English Lop exhibitors have their own special way of cleaning the inside of the ears. The method employed is always the same no matter what solution is used to clean with and should be carried out with the lop placed on a grooming table, allowed to settle and be calm.

If the lop was cleaned correctly as a youngster then the leather of the ear should

Off to the show

not be really dirty and a quick wipe with something like E45 cream on a cotton wool pad should remove any accumulated grime. The leather of the ear should then be folded over to allow a good view right down into the ear. Cotton buds soaked in something like surgical spirit can then be used to get right down into all the folds in the ear and make sure that they are all spotless.

Some exhibitors would rather use an oil based solution like Baby Oil, however whilst this will undoubtedly clean the ear, extreme care must be taken not to get the oil on the coat as the stain that it will leave is very difficult to remove especially if you are having a last-minute clean the day before a show.

Obviously this is a very delicate task and one that must be carried out very carefully so as not to injure the ear. If the lop has not been shown for a long time and is not in show condition then the ears may be quite dirty. In this case it is best to do the job a little at a time over two or three days as too much pressure on the delicate surface of the ears will cause the blood vessels just below the surface to break and give the ears a blooded appearance that will take many days to repair.

An important part of preparing a lop for showing is training it to either sit in the required pose for the breed or more importantly to just behave itself whilst it is on the table and whilst the Judge is handling it.

Of course there is no official requirement for the lop to be trained for the show table but one that misbehaves itself or is too difficult for the Judge to handle does not show itself to its best, whereas one that just sits there in the required pose shouts at the Judge 'look at me'.

Training should begin at a very early age, albeit very gently. If the young lops are regularly handled from about six weeks of age they will be ready for training from about ten weeks old.

It is best to start by letting them run around on a grooming table to get them used to being free but within a confined area. Start by just stroking them and getting them used to you restricting their movement. In no time at all the majority of young lops will sit at peace and allow you to stroke them and once they are happy with this then you can start 'coupling' them in.

Coupling is where the back end is tucked in so that they have a short cobby appearance as required by the standard. As this is a comfortable position for all the lops they readily accept it. Coupling in is easily achieved: as your hand strokes over the back just bring your hand around the rump and tuck it under the body.

All of the lops except the English are required to sit up on their front legs; the Miniature Lop should sit right up to show off its strong front legs and well developed chest whereas the Dwarf, French, German, Cashmere and Mini Cashmere and Meissner lops should sit half up so that the head is raised off the table to show off the crown of the head and the head back into the shoulders so that no neck is seen. These may sound quite artificial positions but they show off the attributes that the Judge wants to see and disguise the ones that he does not want to see.

A lop that has been trained correctly will sit for a long time in the correct position with the minimum of handling by the stewards.

Above, Bradford Championship Show, held annually each January, is the Fancy's largest all-breeds rabbit show. Fanciers are awaiting the "best in show" announcement.
Inset: A Dwarf Lop is judged alongside an Angora in the Ladies Grand Challenge

Throughout the training period you should frequently turn the lop over on its back and handle its feet and check its teeth so that it becomes used to it and is not troubled by it when the Judge does it.

A lop must learn when it is time for serious business and when it is time for playing. Perhaps the worse thing you can do when training a lop is to have it jumping up on your shoulder and having cuddles, as there is a very good chance this is exactly what it will do with the Judge.

With English Lops you should use a 'yard stick' and measure the length and width of the ears frequently when they are young, as they will be measured every time they are shown and should be accustomed to the procedure.

Another tactic employed by most exhibitors is to take the young lop for a few short trips in the car before their first show. Rabbits are, generally speaking, very adaptable animals and as such will soon become accustomed to a travel box and the car as they quickly learn that they do come home to their normal surroundings when the show is over. Like the training of any animal, little and often with a great deal of patience and TLC are all that is required.

One thing for certain, nobody shows rabbits to make money; it is highly unlikely that your prize money will equal or exceed your entry fee to the show. This does not take into account all the other costs that running a stud and getting your lops to a show will cost you.

Exhibiting lops is very much like most hobbies, it depends on how much you want to put into it and how much it is going to cost you. There is no doubt that those at the top of this wonderful hobby spend an awful lot of money just on travelling to shows the length and breadth of the country, but they see it as money well spent as they get the results that their efforts deserve.

For the majority of Fanciers who only show at their local shows and one or two of the big shows a year it is still a considerable investment for which you can be certain there will be very little financial reward. But the friendship, camaraderie, and delight at winning with a lop that you have bred are worth far more than money can buy.

Chapter 7
The Cashmere Lop

*Red Eyed Whites are the most popular Cashmeres. Adult buck (above)
and his under five months son exhibited by Mrs Maureen Faint*

Black. Exhibited by Mrs M Brand

Sooty Fawn. Exhibited by Miss Sophie Mitchell

Agouti. Exhibited by Mr S Whincup

Siamese Sable. Exhibited by Mrs M Faint

Seal Point. (Fur & Feather photo library)

Orange (Fur & Feather photo library)

History

It would appear that the very first Cashmere Lops were long-haired genetic mutations of the Dwarf Lop. It is impossible to put a date on when the first Cashmere Lop was bred as it is almost certain that many were culled out of Dwarf Lop litters by the breeders as unwanted deformities of the Dwarf Lop.

We do know that by the early 1980's Mrs L A Plant applied to the Rare Variety Club to have the breed accepted under the name 'Thistledown'. This name was rejected on the grounds that it sounded too much like a stud name.

By the mid 1980's the National Cashmere Lop Club was formed and following the work of a dedicated band of followers the B.R.C. accepted a Breed Standard. The original Breed Standard was to stay in force for some ten years until some slight alterations were made in 1996 when the present day Breed Standard was accepted.

In 1986 just one Cashmere Lop was exhibited at the Bradford Championship Show. Five years later in 1991 the figure had risen to 67, a truly remarkable increase in such a short space of time. Whilst the numbers exhibited since have never quite reached the 1991 peak they have remained consistently high with more Cashmere Lops being exhibited at all the Bradford Championship Shows since then than English, French, Meissner or German Lops.

Special Care

Whilst the special care required to keep an adult Cashmere Lop in a healthy condition is not particularly onerous, one should consider carefully before your purchase what is involved in keeping these beautiful long-coated lops.

The young Cashmere Lop is perhaps the most demanding as the youngster's coat requires a lot of grooming; it is recommended that a grooming session of 10 minutes a day is required to introduce the lop to the stresses of being groomed.

Within two or three weeks of commencing the 10 minute a day grooming sessions the lop should be sufficiently accustomed to grooming to accept the gradual introduction of grooming sessions of about 20 minutes a day.

As the Cashmere Lop develops its adult coat then the grooming sessions can be reduced gradually to a twice weekly 20-30 minute session and eventually to a weekly session of about 30 minutes.

In fact the full-coated adult that is not in moult and not being exhibited will require little more than a monthly check of the chest and genital areas if it is from good stock and has the correct coat. This may all sound like an awful lot of work but anyone contemplating keeping the breed should not only be aware of the requirements but be prepared to spend the required time grooming.

There are certainly numerous wrong ways to groom a Cashmere

Lop but there is probably no one right way as every breeder has a slight variation on how it should be done.

If the lop does not feel safe and secure then it will not sit still and allow you to groom it. It is best to sit on a stool or box so that the upper part of your legs are parallel with the floor; and provide a flat and stable grooming platform to sit the lop on. The lop should

Grooming a young Cashmere. (Photo from The Beginner's Guide to the Cashmere Lop, published by Coney Press)

then be sat on the groomer's legs so that it faces towards the body.

Using a cat dematting comb (the kind that has alternate long and short teeth) start at the tail and gently tease out any loose hair. The hand not holding the comb should be used to work the coat from tail to head so that the coat is lifted allowing the long teeth of the comb to gently tease out the coat.

Under no circumstances should the comb be used to pull out any knots; the rabbit's skin is very thin and therefore tears easily. The fingers must be used to break the knot apart before the comb can be used to gently remove the knotted hair. This work must be continued across the back and sides of the lop and up to the neck.

To groom the underside of the Cashmere Lop it should be turned on its back so that its back legs are towards and resting against the groomer's stomach and its back rests comfortably between the legs. The same technique as was used on the back is employed on the underside with extreme care being exercised in the area of the genitals.

Of course the best way to learn the specialist techniques required to groom a Cashmere Lop is at the hands of an experienced breeder and exhibitor.

The Cashmere Lop is the same size as the Dwarf Lop and therefore has similar housing requirements; like the Dwarf Lop they should be kept in hutches with solid floors as being kept permanently on wire floors will lead to sore hocks. Whilst wood shavings are undoubtedly the best floor covering for Dwarf Lops this is not the case with the Cashmere Lop as the shavings will become embedded in the long fur and cause even more knotting than would occur naturally. Cashmere Lops are best bedded on heavy sawdust; that is to say sawdust that is not fine and full of dust but is heavy enough to fall through one's fingers. If the lop is white or has white feet then the sawdust must be white otherwise it will stain the feet.

Showing

Showing Cashmere Lops is really no different to showing any other lops as they are hardy animals and will readily adapt to the rigours of showing. However, they must be thoroughly prepared before the show and unlike other lops that can be taken from their pens, given a quick dust down and exhibited, the preparation of the Cashmere Lop for exhibition will take time and experience.

Time, because the grooming process must be 'little and often'

and experience, because all too often the results of over zealous and inexperienced grooming are manifested in the poorly presented, semi-bald Cashmere Lop that is seen all too often on the show bench.

At shows Cashmere Lops are penned differently to all the other lops, as they are always placed on wire covered stands and never on sawdust or shavings.

The stands are an 8inch x 17inch wooden frame that is covered with wire. Each lop requires two. As the standard show pen is 18inches x 18inches a single frame of this size would not fit through the door opening, however two halves will fit through the opening and then come together to form a whole. Most exhibitors also have wire stages built into their travelling boxes to prevent a week's preparation for a show being ruined by soiling on the way to the show.

Cashmere Lops should never have other rabbits housed above them at shows as the shavings on which another breed of rabbit is bedded could, and almost certainly will, fall from an upper pen into a pen below it, thus ruining all the hours spent preparing for the show. Cashmere Lop exhibitors should, and have every right to, insist that their lops are penned in the top pens.

The final leg of getting the Cashmere Lop into the Judge's hands in immaculate condition should also be handled by the owner personally if a last minute disaster is to be avoided. All too often a rabbit will have messed on the judging table and the first action of the stewards is to grab a handful of shavings and rub it into the offending deposit to absorb it. Invariably the stewards will then leave shavings on the judging table so that no other rabbit dirties itself on the residue, but of course the shavings can cause the Cashmere Lop exhibitor just as much trouble as the remains of what the other rabbit deposited on the table. The only sure way to avoid this potentially disastrous situation is to steward your lop yourself.

Although the Cashmere Lop was derived from the Dwarf Lop for some reason it seems to excel type; many exhibits are seen with better heads and shoulders than their Dwarf cousins.

Another anomaly is that the adult Cashmere Lop does seem to retain their shape far better than Dwarf and Miniature Lops and it is not uncommon for the winning Cashmere Lop to be a doe, something that would be extremely unlikely with the other lops.

Whilst a Cashmere Lop is yet to win the major honours at the Bradford or London Championships shows it can surely only be a matter of time as they are regularly amongst the winners at lesser shows. A well prepared, full-coated Cashmere Lop that excels type is a magnificent animal that can hold its own against the stiffest of competition.

The Cashmere Lop Breed Standard

Ring Size D	Points
1. Body and Condition	30
2. Head, Ears and Crown	30
3. Coat	30
4. Colour	10
Total	100

1. Body and Condition –Short compact and strongly muscled with well rounded loins and broad shoulders giving a compact appearance. The legs should be short, strong and straight.

2. Head, Ears and Crown – The head should be strong, bold and broad with well developed cheeks. There should be no visible neck. The ears are broad, thick, well furred and rounded at the ends. They are carried close to the cheeks giving a horseshoe like shape when viewed from the front. The inside of the ears should not be visible from any angle when carried correctly. The crown, which is the basal ridge of each ear, should be prominent across the top of the skull. The eyes should be bold and bright.

3. Coat – Fur is dense, even and silky with plenty of undercoat approximately 3.81 to 5.08cm (1 ½ to 2 ins) long and should not be woolly, matted or felted. The topcoat is longer and heavier than the undercoat with plenty of longer guard hairs hanging down naturally. Evenness is more important than length.

Weight - The maximum weight is 2.381kgs (5lbs 4ozs) with the ideal weight being 2.15kg (4lbs 12ozs). The minimum adult weight is 1.81kg (4lbs).

Faults - White hairs in solid colours. White toenails in coloured exhibits.

Disqualifications- Over maximum weight,2.381kgs (5lbs 4ozs). Adults under 1.81kgs (4lbs). Waviness in coat, Malocclusion, Deformities.

Interpretation of the Standard

As one would expect, the Cashmere Lop breed standard bears a striking resemblance to that of the Dwarf Lop. Some minor alterations have been made to increase the emphasis on coat; somewhat strangely 'condition' is included with 'body' for 30 points and yet apart from the term 'strongly-muscled with well-rounded loins and broad shoulders' no mention is made of the 'condition' required by the Judge when allocating these 30 points.

With a total of 30 points allocated for the 'head, ears and crown' great emphasis is put on the head of the Cashmere Lop and, as was stated earlier, this really does appear to be an area that the Cashmere breeders have succeeded in as the quality Cashmere Lops that win at the shows certainly do excel in the head and ear departments.

Of all the lop breeds the Cashmere Lops display the broadest and flattest heads and when this magnificent head is encompassed by a pair of broad, thick, well rounded ears that form a horseshoe shape then surely there can be no more pleasing sight.

Within the Cashmere Lop breed standard 30 points are allocated to coat. This is really no different from the 20 points for coat and 10 points for guard hairs allocated in the Dwarf Lop breed standard, it just means that the 10 points for guard hairs are included in the total of 30 points. Therefore, like the Dwarf Lop there are almost a third of all points allocated for coat, albeit a very different coat to that of the Dwarf Lop.

The Cashmere coat is what makes the breed stand out from all others and whilst the coat should be between 1 ½ inches and 2 inches in length it is evenness that is more important than length. Many of the early Cashmere Lops had woolly coats but thanks to the perseverance of the Cashmere Lop breeders and many years of selective breeding these woolly coats are now rarely seen. The ideal adult Cashmere Lop should have a very slightly coarse feeling to the top coat when stroked from the shoulders downward; the undercoat should be silky, giving the dense, even, silky coat required by the breed standard.

The range of colours that Cashmere Lops are now seen in is also a testament to the dedication of those that have worked on the breed for many years. Whilst the early specimens were mainly agouti in colour the full range of colours can now be seen and any colour

recognised by the B.R.C. can almost certainly be found in some fancier's shed being 'worked on'.

With 10 points available for colour those exhibits that adhere to the requirements of the colour may just gain the edge and could well make the difference between first or second or even winning and losing. Therefore 'true' colour breeding is imperative for those who aspire to producing a winner.

The Cashmere Lop is subject to the same faults and

disqualifications as all the other lops with one extra fault added into the breed standard that is specific to the Cashmere Lop. 'Waviness in coat' is a trait that is believed to come from the astrex gene and is undesirable in the Cashmere Lop. Any animals showing this trait should be removed from the breeding programme as their use would be deleterious to all the good work that has been put into producing the excellent silky coats that are seen today.

Whilst the Cashmere Lop has never gained the same popularity as its close relation the Dwarf Lop, perhaps because of its grooming requirements, it is nevertheless a popular exhibition rabbit consistently winning at Open Shows.

In fact in 1999 the Cashmere Lop recorded more Open Show wins (7) than the English Lop(5) and the French Lop (1) so whilst it may never be the most popular lop on the show bench it does have a dedicated band of followers who are prepared to put in the time and effort required to take this stunning breed to the very top of the table.

Chapter 8
The Dwarf Lop

The Agouti and Red Eyed White are popular Dwarf Lop colourss.
Above: Agouti exhibited by Mr K Wakefield.
Below: REW exhibited by Mr N Jefferis

Chinchilla. Exhibited by Bunny Barn Stud

Black. (Fur & Feather Photo Library)

Sable. Exhibited by Mr G Coote

Fawn. Exhibited by Mrs M Embry

Butterfly. Exhibited by R & D Colon

Otter. Exhibited by Mr & Mrs Gay

Sooty Fawn.
Exhibited by Mr W Parish

History

It would be easy to say that the Dwarf Lop is just a scaled down version of the French Lop, however, it is how this scaling down was achieved that not only differentiates the two breeds but also accounts for another major difference, colour and coat.

Much more emphasis is put on coat and condition in the Dwarf Lop breed standard than in the French Lop breed standard and there are many more colours in the Dwarf Lop than there are in the French Lop.

The French Lop was indeed the basis for the Dwarf Lop but it was crossed with the Chinchilla and the Netherland Dwarf to reduce the size rather than just selectively breeding small French Lops for numerous generations. It was the use of the Netherland Dwarf that accounts for the great variety of colours in Dwarf Lops today.

Known as the Klein (Little) Widder (Hanging Ear) the Dwarf Lop that had been developed in Holland during the 1950's was first seen by British fanciers at the Utrecht Show in 1968. In 1970 George Scott was the first to import them into Britain.

Many of the early specimens grew too large and had poor ear carriage and as their arrival in Britain was only just before the Ministry ban on the importation of rabbits much credit is due to the few British fanciers who worked on the breed.

At the formation of the National French and Dwarf Lop Club in 1977 the problems with weight were so acute that the members of the Club asked the B.R.C. for a larger ring. The request was refused and the breeders just had to work on bringing the size and weight down. Meanwhile the Dutch fanciers had continued to work on size and type and it was Angio Chiesa who imported eight of these much improved small lops in 1978, even though he lost some of them while they were in quarantine.

The Chiesa lops were not to everyone's liking. Some were so small as to be below the three and a half pounds required by the standard; however, Chiesa exhibited some of his lops at the Club's Adult Stock Show at Coventry in 1979 and was awarded Best in Show with one of them.

This was to prove the turning point for the breed as in 1980 a Dwarf Lop did well in the Fancy Challenge at the Bradford

Championship Show and by 1981 Dwarf Lops were winning Best in Show at open shows and in fact were exceeding French Lops in some areas.

Although the numbers of Dwarf Lops have declined in recent years, perhaps in response to the rise in popularity of the Miniature Lop, they were for many years the

Dwarf Lop exhibited by Mr K Brockhill at the 1979 Bradford Championship Show

most popular lop exhibited. They reached their highest number at the Bradford Championship Show in 1996 when 152 were shown, making it the second highest number in any breed shown that year.

Special Care

It would be easy to say that no special care is required for the Dwarf Lop but it would be more accurate to say little special care and a lot of attention to routine maintenance tasks is what is required. If the Dwarf Lop is kept for exhibition then it must be within the weight limit of 5lb 4ozs. If the lop is going to be over the limit when fed on the normal ration then there is nothing that can be done for it.

The keeper of Dwarf Lops must be a careful observer of stock and through observation learn each individual lop's food requirements. A lop should be kept lean and fit and should be firm and well muscled to the touch with no bagginess in the coat around the rear end; this can only be achieved through correct feeding.

Most adult lops are fed once a day and usually at night on either pellets or a dry mix, this should be supplemented with plenty of sweet smelling hay and fresh water. This strict attention to feeding is as equally important for the breeding doe as it is for exhibition lops; overweight does will be reluctant to mate and are more likely to have birthing problems or give birth to dead kits.

Dwarf Lops should not be housed in wire cages as the fur on their feet is not particularly thick and any system of bedding other than a deep layer of wood shavings will almost certainly result in sore or bald hocks. Once the hocks are bald it is notoriously difficult to restore hair growth. The hocks can become calloused; bald or calloused hocks will almost certainly result in the lop being disqualified by a judge on the grounds that it is a marked rabbit.

The Dwarf Lop Breed Standard awards 20 points for 'coat', if these 20 points are added to the percentage of the 30 points allocated for 'type and condition' and the 10 points for guard hairs then it will be seen that the coat and condition of the Dwarf Lop is a major factor on the show table.

All rabbits must moult and because of the high ratio of points allocated for coat and condition Dwarf Lops showing any signs of moult should not be exhibited. Presuming the lop is not in moult then it is only good stockmanship and attention to detail that will get that coat into exhibition condition; the old saying 'what you see on the outside is a reflection of what you put inside' is very true. A shiny, healthy coat can only be achieved through a good feeding regime using quality food.

Showing

Like all lops the Dwarf Lop readily adapts to the rigours of show life if it is trained to accept human handling when young and introduced to a life of travelling and strange pens gradually and sympathetically.

Training a Dwarf Lop for showing is relatively simple if done slowly and with patience. When the lop is young and still with its mother it should be gently stroked along the back and on the head between the eyes every feeding time. This is done so that it becomes accustomed to the smell and feel of the human hand; there is nothing to be gained from trying to get the young kit to sit still in the posed position, this will come later.

Once the kits are separated from their mother then more serious training can commence. Kits should be placed individually on a bench with a non-slip surface, then with a lot of gentle stroking the

lop will learn to sit still.

Once the lop is happy to sit still then it will grow in confidence and when it is confident sitting still it will sit up; it is only the lop that is sitting still with its head up and can show itself off that gets the judges attention.

A nervous lop that sits on the show table hunched up and with its head down on the table will not do itself any favours and will not catch the eye of the judge.

Once the lop is happy and confident when being handled the owner should turn it on its back and check the teeth. Of course you will have checked them when it was young and know that they are perfectly alright, but by going through the motions regularly the lop will become accustomed to having its teeth checked and will not become distressed the first time a judge checks them.

Similarly the owner should handle the young lop's feet and gently pull each front leg out in turn and blow into the fur across the chest and in the armpits as this is exactly what a judge will do and being accustomed to it could prevent a disaster.

In order to introduce the young Dwarf Lop to show life it should first become accustomed to short periods of time in a travelling box and then to short car journeys in the travelling box. Hopefully the exhibitor can find a small show near to home to introduce the young lop to show life; this will acclimatise the youngster gently and not put it off showing.

Whilst none of the above may sound special to the Dwarf Lop it is worth remembering that there are an awful lot of points within the breed standard of the Dwarf Lop that are allocated for coat and condition and that no rabbit can show off its coat and condition if it is so stressed or nervous on the table that the Judge cannot assess it properly.

The Dwarf Lop Breed Standard

Ring size C	Points
1. General type and condition	30
2. Head, Ears, Crown and Eyes	25
3. Coat	20
4. Guard Hairs	10
5. Colour	15
Total	100

1. **Type -** Body short with well-rounded loins. Deep chest and wide shoulders, giving a cobby well-muscled appearance. Short strong legs.

2. **Head, Crown, Ears and Eyes**

Head – Well developed particularly in bucks. Good width between eyes. Full cheeks and broad muzzle are desirable.

Crown – The basal ridge of the ears should appear prominent across the top of the skull.

Ears – Should be broad, thick well-furred and rounded at the ends. They should be carried close to the cheeks giving a horse-shoe like outline when viewed from the front. The inside of the ears should not be visible from any angle when carried correctly. The ears are not measured.

Eyes – Round and bright.

3. **Coat** – Coat to be dense and of good length, rollback with an abundance of guard hairs.

4. **Guard Hairs** – An abundance of guard hairs.

5. **Colour** – Any colour or pattern that conforms to the colour or pattern of recognised breeds.

Weight –Maximum - 5lb 4oz
      Minimum – 4lb 4oz

Faults – Narrow shoulders, long in body, narrow head. Ears carried back or not fully lopped. Coat too short or fly-back. Excessive white hairs in coloured exhibits, light tails in sooties. White tails in sooties a serious fault.

Disqualifications – Weight over maximum. Poor condition. Malocclusion. Runny eyes, odd coloured or walleyes. Putty nose. Bunches of white hairs or white toenails in coloured exhibits.

Interpretation of the Standard

With one exception little has changed in the Dwarf Lop Breed Standard since it was first accepted by the B.R.C. in 1977. There was some consolidation of the wording but following a vote by the members of the National French and Dwarf Lop Club in 2000 a minimum weight of 4 pounds 4 ounces was introduced.

This is actually quite a major change when one looks back at the original Breeds Standard and sees that the minimum weight laid down then was 3 pounds and 8 ounces. A change of over 20% in the minimum weight has meant that the members are demanding that the Dwarf Lop must now be well muscled, strong, sturdy animals but of course must not exceed the same maximum weight that was laid down all those years ago.

Within the weight limits (4lb 4oz – 5lb 4oz) the breeder of the Dwarf Lop must present a cobby rabbit that has a short body, is well muscled with broad shoulders and has short strong legs. In other words, a power pack of a rabbit. The quality Dwarf Lop that has these attributes is indeed an imposing sight.

Having produced the Dwarf Lop with the required body type and within the imposed weight limits the breeder must then consider the attributes required of the head, for surely it is the magnificent full cheeks and broad muzzle required of the adult buck that make the Dwarf Lop a show winner.

The broad, flat-faced head must be surmounted by a prominent

'crown', this ridge stands out across the top of the head between the base of the ears and frames the front view of the head. To complete the view of the head the ears should hang close to the sides of the head forming a horse-shoe shape so that no part of the inside of the ears can be seen from any direction. Whilst the ears of the Dwarf Lop are not measured when it is being judged they must be sufficiently long to hang correctly.

In the original Breed Standard of 1977 a total of 40 points was allocated to the combination of coat, guard hairs and colour; the present standard allows 45 point for these elements. This change further emphasises the importance put on the coat. It is the balance of guard hairs that makes the subtle difference between a good coat and the exceptional one required of a winning Dwarf Lop.

If you watch a Judge when he is assessing a Dwarf Lop you will see that he takes some of the fur on the lop's back between his thumb and forefinger and then gets his eyes down level with the lop's back so that he can see the guard hairs that are protruding above the undercoat.

The guard hairs are particularly prominent in agoutis, which is why the agoutis usually have the best coats, with the best roll back and why the agoutis usually win at shows. Of course the shaded and tan patterns must have good guard hairs for it is their presence that makes the coat, however some of the selfs suffer from a lack of guard hairs and therefore are the most difficult to get 'into coat'.

Unlike the other Lops, the Dwarf Lops have the advantage that they were bred down to size using the Netherland Dwarf and the Chinchilla which accounts for the great variety of colours in the breed. Much credit must be given to the Dwarf Lop breeders who have worked on the breeding of true colours over the years. With 15 points for colour it can be seen that any Dwarf Lop that does not display true colour will not win at the top level.

For some inexplicable reason no Dwarf Lop has ever won either the London or Bradford Championship Show, this is somewhat surprising as they are without question magnificent animals when they excel type and are in full coat. Perhaps it is the high standard that the Dwarf Lop breeders have imposed on themselves by putting so much emphasis on coat and condition that makes it so difficult to attain the very highest level of perfection.

Although the Dwarf Lop has declined in popularity in recent years there are still many dedicated breeders of Dwarf Lops across the country who are determined that one day, in the not too distant future, a Dwarf Lop will come out above all others at a five star Championship Show.

Chapter 9
The English Lop

Phil Wheeler's English Lop achieved best in show at the 2001 Bradford Championship Show; below the author's Salix Stud was best of breed in 2002

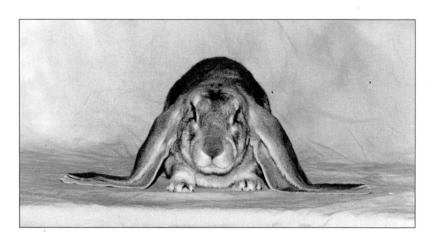

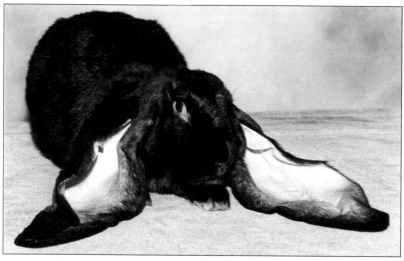

In 2002 Phil Wheeler's English Lop was measured by judge Fred Clipsham
and entered the Guinness Book of Records as the lop with the largest ear span.
Below: Mrs M Cawdron's White

History

The first evidence we have of the English Lop is in 16th century European tapestries that displayed large grey rabbits with ears that lopped. However, it was not until the nineteenth century that the English Lop came to prominence as a Fancy exhibition rabbit.

'Lop Eared Rabbit' from the cover of an 1883 magazine
"Poultry, Pigeons, Cage Birds, Rabbits"

First mentioned by Mowbray in 1822 the English Lop really started to be noticed around the 1850's.

It was in 1850 that George Powell of the Chatham and Rochester Fancy Rabbit Club had his grey buck and black and white doe featured in the Greater London Area newspaper. These two lops were measured at about 21½ inches x 5 inches.

Although the first Lop Standard was drafted in 1850 it was the two standards that were published in 1875 that were to form the basis of the standard that we know today. Both Mr J Newman's and Mr Millington's version of the standard put most emphasis on ear length although the Newman standard allocated 25 points for length and 20 for width whilst the Millington standard (marked out of a total of 14 points) gave 4 points for length and only 1 point for width. Both of these standards did require the lop to have ears that 'tapered small at the end' suggesting that they desired a tapered ear, the opposite of today's 'well rounded at the tips'.

Full Lop

Oar Lop

In 1860 four types of lop were recognised other than the 'natural' lop. The Oar Lop – with ear carriage at 45 degrees and ears

Horn Lop

rising with body movement; the Half Lop – with ears falling to one side; the Horned Lop – with ears falling forward over the face and eyes; and the Flat Lop – with ears going upwards from the ear base, forming a crown and sweeping down and forward.

Quite why none of these varieties survived is hard to say; one can only surmise that the variants were in fact only traits that are often seen in young or poorly developed lops and that they were not true genetic traits that could be bred for.

By November 16, 1863 the English Lop had enough presence to be featured on the cover of *Fur & Feather* when a fawn lop, City Wonder, owned by T Wallace was judged at Bath by a Mr Jennings and measured at over 28 inches.

For the next fifty or so years great emphasis was placed on ear length and there are many stories of the terrible cruelty that was inflicted on the lops to increase the length of the ears.

Half Lop

Most of this cruelty centred on keeping them in very hot conditions, often bake houses or unventilated sheds that were further heated with paraffin stoves.

The early lops had been huge creatures, often exceeding 20 pounds in weight, however, the methods employed by breeders in their quest to increase ear length bought about the decline in the vitality of the lop. They suffered terribly with snuffles and lung diseases; they could not be shown at outdoor shows because they had been kept in such hot conditions that they could not stand the cold, and their decline in popularity was inevitable.

London was the centre of the English Lop during the 19th century but many lops were exported throughout the world, in particular to America; there are reports of a class being put on for English Lops at the 1869 Sacramento State Fair in California and it is reported that a famous buck 'Robin Hood' was exported to the U.S.A at the turn of the century for $200.

It was probably about 1900 that the Lop reached its highest point in popularity and quality. In 1901, Captain Youlton broke all records when his six month old fawn buck was measured at 30 1/8 inches by 7 3/8 inches at Warminister; a record only recently surpassed by Phil Wheeler's two year old black English Lop buck Toby the Third which was measured at 30 ¼ inches by 7 3/4 by judge Fred Clipsham at Sheffield in June 2002.

In 1910, 94 English Lops were exhibited at the National English Lop Club show at Leamington, a number that is never likely to be seen again; by the end of the century things had got so bad that only one English Lop was exhibited at the 1998 Bradford Championship Show.

The Bradford Championship Show has been won four times in its 82 year history by English Lops. In 1932 and 1934 A Pedlar triumphed, whilst in 1945 Busset's lop took the honours. It then took another fifty six years before Phil Wheeler's sooty buck 'Star' won in 2001.

With the rise in popularity of all the other lops and the trend toward smaller rabbits in general, the English Lop is unlikely to ever recover to its former numbers and it is likely to remain in the hands of a few dedicated followers to keep the breed alive. Some European countries have now introduced rules disqualifying lops over a certain ear length and breeders are concentrating on improving ear texture and body size, thus removing the challenge of improving the overall package.

The future of the magnificent English Lop, the King of the Fancy, is anybody's guess. Their unique temperament and placid nature; the fact that they have no fear of other household pets and their love for their owners that borders on devotion does make them ideally suited as pets, and in fact as house-rabbits.

They are prolific breeders that require no courtship prior to being mated; the does often producing huge litters of ten or eleven. Whilst there will always be a market for youngsters, realistically even the most ardent supporter of the breed would find it difficult to be too optimistic.

Special Care

Perhaps one of the reasons why the English Lop is not very popular in the twenty first century is that it does require some special care.

It is, for instance the only exhibition rabbit in Britain that is

English Lop house pet

allowed to have its toe nails cut as an under five months old. The nails must be cut on a regular basis whilst the kittens are still with their mother and throughout their lives as long and sharp toe-nails are the cause of more ear damage than anything else.

Small nicks in the ears of very young kits may well heal over as they get older, but a tear or piece missing will not heal and will mean that the lop will not be able to be shown. Although the young lops' ears stop growing at 14 weeks of age they are fairly thin at this age and are easily damaged.

English Lops have a very thin coat and thus should not be allowed to get unduly cold in the winter. They should always be housed on

The nails must be cut on a regular basis whilst the kittens are still with their mother

a deep layer of shavings that is then covered with straw. This will not only keep them warm in cold weather but will also prevent bald hocks. The dual effect of carrying most of its weight on its back end and a thin coat makes the English Lop highly susceptible to bald hocks that will obviously lose it points when being judged.

It should be noted that English Lops should also be bedded on deep shavings and straw when they are penned at shows. The damage caused by a rough board in a pen could take many months to repair.

The large ears of the English Lop require surprisingly little special care. When the lop is young and still housed with its mother, brothers and sisters there is little that can be done other than keeping nails short. Once the litter is separated then each lop's ears should be thoroughly cleaned. It is important to always keep the lops ears clean as it is only in clean ears that any disease can be spotted at an early stage and treated.

As the ears thicken up with age there should be few problems with them. If the ears are kept clean and are checked regularly when the routine health check is carried out, there really should be few problems.

Surprisingly an English Lop's ears stop growing at the age of 14 weeks; even more surprisingly you can fairly accurately calculate the final length and width of the lops ears from as young as four weeks of age.

Using the chart below you measure the length and width of the ears at two-week intervals from four weeks of age and simply add the figure in the chart. So that a lop measured at, say, six weeks of age and found to be 20 inches in length by 4¾ inches in width should, if all goes well, achieve an adult ear measurement of 27 x 6 ½ inches.

Age	Length	Age	Width
4 weeks	+12inches	4 weeks	+2 ½inches
6 weeks	+7inches	6 weeks	+1 ¾inches
8 weeks	+5inches	8 weeks	+1inch
10 weeks	+3inches	10 weeks	¾inches
12 weeks	+2inches	12 weeks	¼inches
14 weeks	+1inch		

When mating English Lops the 'assisted' method of mating must always be used as the weight of an amorous buck jumping onto a doe can cause severe spinal problems for the doe.

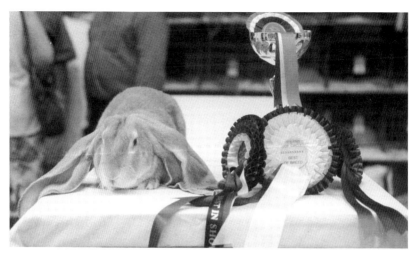

Author's 6 month old English Lop (28x7) winning the West Midland Championship Show 2003

Showing

The young English Lop, whilst not delicate, must be treated with respect; the timing of the young lop's first show must be chosen carefully as must the venue and if possible the judge.

English Lops come into their intermediate (or teenage) coat at about 13 to 14 weeks and if the right show and judge can be found this is a good time to show them; any younger and the lop will not be in coat and is also likely to be set back in its development by the stress induced by showing it.

A local show is ideal for the lop's first show as it will mean a short time in a travelling box and hopefully a fairly short day. If a local show can be found when the lop is about 13 weeks old and the show is being judged by an English Lop panel judge then so much the better.

Most judges can handle English Lops as they really are no different to any other large rabbit. However, an English Lop panel judge will be very experienced at handling and assessing English Lops and will not only give you a more accurate assessment of the lop's attributes but also see the detail that a non-specialist judge might well miss.

Having shown the lop at 13 -14 weeks it will almost certainly then start moulting to grow its adult coat and therefore become unsuitable for showing for some considerable time. The adolescent lop may well come into full adult coat by about 6 months of age. However, it must then be shown as an adult and will not be developed enough to compete against more mature animals so will probably not be ready for showing until eight or nine months of age.

From what has been said above it can be seen that you may well only be able to show an English Lop once or twice in the first nine months of its life. Having said that you should then get a show life through to about two years of age by which time the quality of the coat will start to deteriorate and is unlikely to recover again to a standard that is good enough for the show bench.

English lops should sit 'down' on the show table, that is to say they should sit with their shoulders down and their front legs straight out in front of them. The back end should then be coupled in; this combination of low shoulders and coupled back end accentuates the mandolin shape that is required in the exhibition English Lop. Once a lop learns to sit comfortably in this position little else is required in its handling on the show table other than that the steward should put their arms down the sides of the lop and hold its shoulders whilst the Judge is measuring the ears; this prevents the lop moving and allows the judge to get an accurate measurement.

Because of the size of the ears all stewards handling English Lops on the show bench must be aware of other rabbits on the table as there could be nothing worse than to see the magnificent ears of an English Lop damaged for life by one quick bite from another rabbit.

English Lop Breed Standard

	Ring size H	Points
1.	Ear Length	10
2.	Ear Width	15
3.	Ear Shape	15
4.	Ear Substance and Carriage	10
5.	Colour and Markings	10
6.	Type	10
7.	Straight Feet and Tail	10

8.	Eyes	5
9.	Size	10
10.	Condition	5
	Total	100

1. **Ear Length.**
2. **Ear Width.**
3. **Ear Shape** – To be well rounded at the tips, not trowel shaped.
4. **Ear Substance and Carriage** – To be nice and thick like leather, not like thin paper, not to be carried pricked in any way; no pimples.
5. **Colour and Markings** – Any colour permitted, but whatever colour it must be good i.e. black to be raven black, fawn, rich golden fawn, sooty-fawn, shading to be dense. See footnote re marked rabbits.
6. **Type** – The head to be bold, the whole body of the rabbit to resemble a mandolin, curved side uppermost.
7. **Straight Feet and Tail** – The front feet not to be bow legged or bent, tail not to be screwed.
8. **Eyes**- To be bold and bright, not dull.
9. **Size** – As large as possible, but not out of proportion.
10. **Condition** – Firm in flesh, good in coat, no ear canker or any other disease.

FOOTNOTE: Marked specimens can be of any of these colours. The white markings around the nose to be such that leave a distinct butterfly smut or as the shadings on the Sooty-Fawn. The white should extend upwards from the chin and chest over the shoulder with two spots, one each side of the shoulders called shoulder spots. No white to be present in the general body colouring. The belly to be white and similar to the tan on the Tan rabbit but not brindled up the sides of the body.

Interpretation of the Standard
English Lops are unique among the lops in that their show classes are not divided by colour but rather by ear length, therefore at smaller shows you may well only have one class for all ear lengths irrespective of colour whilst at the major championship shows there could be as

many as five different ear length classes. It is therefore important that an English Lop owner can measure their own lops' ears accurately and know which classes to enter them in. As will be seen in the standard, ear length is only allocated 10 points so whilst all English Lop breeders seem to put an inordinate emphasis on length, width and shape are actually far more important with 15 points for each. As a general rule the length of the ears should be four times the width, so that a 28inch lop should have 7inch wide ears.

The standard requires the ears 'to be well rounded at the tips, not trowel shaped'. This is very hard to describe and can really only be seen when a really good lop is compared with a lesser one. The ear substance and carriage is worth 10 points on the standard but this is probably an understatement as even the longest eared lop will be heavily penalised if it has poor substance.

With a total of 50 points, i.e. half of all the points on ears then quite rightly British breeders concentrate much of their breeding effort on ears; however there is another 50 points available and all breeders should work on the elements that comprise those 50 points.

Although English Lops do not have colour classes the colour of the lop should conform to the accepted standard for the colour and with 10 points for colour it actually makes colour just as important as ear length. Similarly for type and size there are 20 points available; the boldness of the head will only come on bucks and only on mature bucks. However, the size and all-important 'mandolin shape' must be bred into the lop.

If an English Lop is positioned correctly with the back end coupled in and the lop down on its shoulders then the back should rise in the mandolin shape and the sides of the lop should also display the curve as in the up-turned mandolin – a straight sided or flat backed English Lop is absolutely no use at all and will be heavily penalised by all judges.

Bent/bowed front legs and skewed tails are a serious fault and are quite rightly penalised by judges. Bowed legs are usually an inherited fault but bent legs can be caused in a fast growing youngster where the bones are just not strong enough to cope with the rapidly increasing weight.

Feeding young lops full fat goats milk will increase their calcium intake and strengthen bones and thus hopefully prevent bent front legs. Tails can be damaged at birth when the dam cleans the newborn kits. Unfortunately this is very hard to detect and might not be discovered until the lop is of sufficient size to check over thoroughly.

The 'condition' of the lop is allocated only 5 points in the standard. This is very surprising and can work against the show lop because whilst a judge can quite rightly pay little heed to the 'condition' when judging the classes as there are only 5 points for it, any lop that is not in exceptional condition will not do well in the challenges. The English Lop that is shown in the peak of condition is a magnificent animal and if it is a good specimen it will do well in the challenges. No matter how good a specimen it is, it will not do well if not in condition.

The new exhibitor of the English Lop must study and learn the standard and then study and, hopefully, handle as many exhibits as possible so that the standard and its interpretation becomes second nature.

Chapter 10
The French Lop

Above: Opal. Exhibitor Astra Stud. Below: RE White. Exhibitor Folly Lops

Steel Butterfly. Exhibited by S & H Elliott

Agouti. Exhibited by Miss C Allcock

Fawn. Exhibited by David Dobbs

Agouti Butterfly. Exhibited by Brian & Jean Lynch

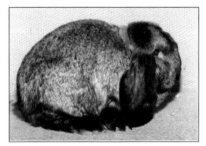

Steel. Exhibited by S & H Elliott

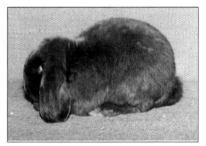

Blue. Exhibited by Pam Hughes

History

Although the history of the French Lop is not entirely clear it is almost certain that it was derived from the English Lop during the nineteenth century. At that time there were four different recognised types of (English) Lop and it is not difficult to see that the French Lop was a shorter eared variant.

M Cordonnier is credited with breeding the first French Lop in

1853 in France, which may seem somewhat odd as London was the centre of Lop breeding at that time. However, it may account for the name, French Lop to differentiate it from 'The Lop' (that was not to become known as the English Lop until the arrival of the French and Dwarf lops in England over 100 years later).

To complicate matters further it was actually the Germans, Dutch and Belgians that were to import the French Lop in the 1860's and then spend much time perfecting them. So an inferior lop type rabbit is bred in France from a cross between the (English) Lop and possibly some form of continental giant breed and then having been named the French Lop is exported to Germany, Holland and Belgium where the breed is developed.

From our point of view the French Lop did not arrive in Britain until 1933 when ten from Holland were exhibited at the old Crystal Palace Show and even then it was dismissed by the exhibitors and judges as. a 'half lop' with ears that barely reached the ground and consequently largely ignored by them. The French Lop was not considered by the judges of the day as worthy of being an exhibition rabbit and it was to continue being bred solely as a meat rabbit.

By the time Meg Brown imported the first French Lop into Britain in 1965 to improve the body on her English Lops, it had become a distinctly different lop, with a bold, broad head that had a 'crown' over the skull. The unique ears of the English Lop had disappeared to be replaced with horseshoe shaped ears that hung close to the cheeks.

These agouti coloured French Lops with their dense coats were imported into Britain from Germany, Belgium and even some from Denmark. Meg Brown also translated the Breed Standard that was accepted by the B.R.C.

This beautiful, massive, thickset lop with its docile nature gained in popularity with exhibitors throughout the 1960's and 70's although it did struggle for acceptance by the judges of the day as it was still considered as an inferior English Lop, with many judges taking a rule and measuring the ear length and width.

Once the National Lop Club took the French and Dwarf Lops under its wing then judges started to appreciate that they were in fact three distinct lops and that they could be judged against each other or any other breed.

However, even though the French Lops were gaining in popularity many felt that the union with the National Lop Club could never do the French (or Dwarf Lop) justice. For one thing the National Lop Club had numerous magnificent trophies to be awarded at its stock shows, but they were nearly all related to ear length and thus not relevant to the French and Dwarf Lops.

Throughout the early 1970's the French Lop steadily increased in popularity with Kathleen Gordon earning the distinction of being the owner of the first French Lop to gain a B.R.C. Gold Star Diploma. The rabbit had in fact been bred by Meg Brown from her original imported stock and Peter Ralphes had the honour of winning the first three star Best in Show with a French Lop. These successes were just the boost that the breed needed but the Government ban on the importation of rabbits meant that stock was becoming very scarce as more and more breeders wanted them.

In 1976 French and Dwarf Lop breeders decided to split from the National Lop Club, and in January 1977 the National French and Dwarf Lop Club was affiliated to the B.R.C. By the end of its first year the newly formed club had held three successful Stock Shows and had a membership of over 100. The membership was to double in the following year as interest in the two breeds increased.

At the first Club Show held at Newark in May 1977 (just four months after the formation of the Club) forty French Lops and six Dwarf Lops were exhibited. Best in Show that day went to a French Lop buck bred by Peter Ralphes – Monsieur D'or. This buck was to go on to win Best of Breed out of sixty exhibits at the London Championship Show later that year and also at the following year's Bradford Championship Show before retiring.

At about the same time as Peter Ralphes was having success Mr Grotchen, a German gentleman living in the south of England, had imported French Lops from his homeland. This was a completely different strain from the Meg Brown-Peter Ralphes rabbit and had massive skulls and lovely type. Mr Grotchen was not an exhibitor and passed his offspring to other fanciers to exhibit.

A third strain was introduced into the 'British' French Lops when Jim Porter imported some excellent stock from Denmark. Although well boned and of very good type and coat they were a little short in the ears and often did not 'lop' correctly. Mr Porter left the Fancy about the time the National French and Dwarf Lop Club was formed and much of his stock was lost to the breed.

However, the three strains – Ralphes (Brown), Grotchen and Porter – are responsible for the magnificent French Lop we see today, with the ear shape, carriage and crown attributed to the Ralphes strain and the magnificent heads, colouring and pattern being a direct result of the influence of the Grotchen strain.

Whilst the French Lop no longer equals the Dwarf Lop in popularity on the show bench and probably never will again it is an extremely popular pet, especially as a house rabbit. Their humorous antics have endeared them to people all over the world; they thrive on attention and just love playing with toys but perhaps their most endearing feature is the way they bond with humans making them totally irresistible.

Special Care

The adult French Lop is a massive animal and may weigh up to 15 or 16lbs. As such it must have sufficient space to live and exercise in; this means at least a six-foot hutch. Because of the French Lop's immense weight it should always be bedded on a deep layer of shavings that has a further layer of barley straw on top of it to prevent sore hocks developing.

The endearing nature of the French Lop does not lend itself to being left in a hutch isolated at the bottom of the garden; this is one rabbit that craves constant human contact. The breeder and exhibitor, who may well keep a lot of French Lops, must have a life style that allows the time each day to spend with these affectionate animals. If they do not get regular human attention they can become quite difficult to handle and as they are very big, powerful lops this would not be a situation any French Lop owner would want to let develop.

To this need for human attention can be added the French Lop's uncanny ability to get on with other animals, particularly other household pets; it is because of this side of their nature that they make such good house rabbits. They just do not seem to bother at all about other animals around them but can certainly look after themselves if another animal attacks them.

Showing

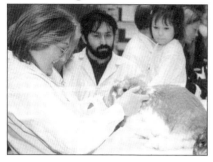

Perhaps the most difficult element to get right when exhibiting French Lops is coat. Because of their dense coat and very thick undercoat they are very difficult to get into full coat with the roll back required by the breed standard; the self-coloureds have less guard hairs than the other colours and thus are even more difficult to get into the prime condition for winning major honours.

Having said that, for the brief spell in any year when they are in full coat they are magnificent animals that can hold their own against any other rabbit.

Perhaps because of the French Lop's size and requirements for human contact they are not the most popular exhibition lop and there are vast areas in Britain where none is exhibited. Conversely there are areas where a lot are exhibited and competition is quite fierce.

This can work both ways; no competition from other French Lops can mean that Club Secretaries are unlikely to book specialist French Lop judges for their shows and therefore the exhibitor will only ever get the opinion of non-specialist judges. Whereas living in an area where a lot of French Lops are exhibited means that the newcomer will constantly be up against very stiff opposition and may quickly become disillusioned.

Somewhat surprisingly the young French Lop is actually slower to develop than the slightly smaller English Lop; whilst an English Lop may be ready for showing at about 12 – 14 weeks this is certainly too young for a French Lop. The stress induced by showing a young French Lop will certainly set back its natural development; it is best left at home until it is at least 4 months old by which time it should be about 8lb in weight and sufficiently developed to take the rigours of showing in its stride.

Showing French Lops presents few problems as they are such amicable rabbits; however, when booking in for shows it is as well to remind the Show Secretary that your lop will require a large pen, preferably a top loading one as there is nothing worse than seeing an inexperienced steward trying to get a French Lop in or out of the front door of a show pen.

Because of their size French Lops should only be handled by experienced stewards and certainly never by children; it may be that you, the French Lop owner should step in and steward your own lops. You may well get accused by other fanciers of 'jockeying' your own rabbits, but the safety of your lops must come first and you can easily avoid this accusation by stewarding all breeds all day.

French Lop Breed Standard

Ring size H	Points
1. Type	30
2. Head, Crown, Ears & Eyes	35
3. Coat	15
4. Condition	10
5. Colour	10
Total	100

1.**Type** – Massive, thickset and firm. The body should be short, broad and well muscled, with little visible neck. The line of the back rises in a curve to a well-muscled rump, which is short and well rounded. The chest is broad and deep providing curved sides where it meets the shoulders, which are broad and strong. The front legs are short, thick and straight. The legs are short, strong, powerful and the hind legs carried parallel to the body. The tail is straight, strong and well furred. A small dewlap is permissible in bucks but is not favourable – dewlaps larger in does.

2.**Head, Crown, Ears and Eyes**

Head: Well developed particularly in bucks. Good width between eyes. Full cheeks and broad muzzle are desirable.

Crown: The basal ridge of the ears should appear prominent across the top of the skull.

Ears: Should be broad, thick, well furred and rounded at the ends. They should be carried close to the cheeks, giving a horseshoe like outline when viewed from the front. The inside of the ears should not visible from any angle when carried correctly. The ears are not measured.

Eyes: Round and bright.

3. Coat – Rollback, dense with plenty of guard hairs. Legs and pads to be well furred.

4. Condition – Condition to be firm and healthy.

5. Colour – Any colour or pattern that conforms to the colour or pattern of recognised breeds.

Weight – As large as possible, minimum adult weight 4.535kgs (10lbs). No maximum weight for adults or u/5 months.

Faults – Poorly muscled, lacking firmness, loose skin over hind legs. Body too long and/or lean. Head not sufficiently characteristic of the breed. Pimpled or damaged ears. Poor ear carriage. Crown not developed. Fly back coat. Bowed or splayed legs. Excessive white hairs in coloured exhibits, white tail in sooty fawn and putty noses (excessive white hairs in nose and top lip).

Disqualifications – Adult weight under 4.535kgs (10lbs). Malocclusion of teeth. White toenails in coloured exhibits. Putty nose.

1994 Bradford Ch Show winner, exhibited by Mrs Jane Williams

Interpretation of the Standard

The standard calls for the French Lop to be as 'large as possible' but it must be made clear that this does not include length. Within the standard it does say that the 'body should be short' and that the 'rump should be well rounded and short'; for exhibition French Lops this shortness is absolutely imperative.

Of course the lop must be massive and powerful with thick legs but it must be compact and not long in the body. With 30 points for type any French Lop that fails in this area has no chance of success on the show bench.

With 35 points for the head, crown, ears and eyes they do score more than type and a well-developed head is an absolute prerequisite for the exhibition lop. This beautiful big head with its full cheeks, broad muzzle and width between the eyes is one of the main distinguishing features between the exhibition and the pet French Lop.

There are still a few snipey, narrow-headed French Lops in Britain; they should certainly be taken out of any serious breeder's breeding programme as they will never do well on the show bench and they should not be exhibited at all.

It is because of the requirement for the French Lop's head to be so well developed that most exhibitors will only show adult bucks. The bucks in all the lop breeds naturally have much broader heads than the does; so whereas this will not be noticeable in under five month exhibits it will in adults and as a general rule only the bucks will be shown.

Of course a young adult doe (maybe between 6-8 months of age) that has all the other requirements of the breed in abundance and is in its first full adult coat and that just happens to be in stunning condition should obviously be shown if the right judge and right show are available.

It is often these young does that do well at Championship Shows where the judges always want their winning rabbits to be in good coat so that they can do well in the challenges and the stunning coat of the young adult may win over an older buck that may have a bigger head and body who is not in such perfect coat.

Like the other flat-faced lops (Dwarf and Miniature) the French Lop suffers from malocclusion. On the show bench this is a disqualification, but any lop suffering from malocclusion should have been eradicated from your stock long before reaching a Judge. This is a hereditary trait and there is only one way to deal with any animals born with it – they must be culled. They should not even be passed on as pets as the animals will lead lives of misery and the owner will lead a life of continually paying vets bills.

There is no doubt that the French Lop is a magnificent beast; its massive bulk and adorable nature will almost certainly endear it to sufficient enthusiasts to perpetuate the breed, even though it is never likely to have the numbers of many of the other more popular lops.

Chapter 11
The German Lop

Above: Agouti Butterfly. Exhibited by Kanichen Stud.

Black. Exhibited by A J Williams

REW. Exhibited by Mrs M Cawdron   *Chinchilla. Exhibited by Mrs R Waring*

Judging a National German Lop show

History

In an attempt to develop a medium size lop, breeders in Germany worked throughout the 1960's to create the German Lop. At this

Agouti. Exhibited by June Parr

time the French Lop at a weight in excess of 10lb and the Holland Lop (to become known in Britain as the Dwarf Lop) weighing between 4 − 5¼lb were the only two flat faced lops.

It is known that the German breeders certainly used the French and the Holland Lop to develop

Mr & Mrs Powell's REW German, best in show at the 1998 London Championship Show

the German Lop but there was also at least one other ingredient in the mix that was to give the German Lop its distinctive Roman nose. Because of the German nose it would be incorrect to say that like the Dwarf Lop it is just another scaled down French Lop in a different weight band.

In Germany the German Lop was officially recognised in 1970 where it was given the name Deutsche Klein Widder. It was imported into Holland in 1972 and gained recognition there in 1976. Although popular in those two countries the breed has not spread widely and may well not have reached Britain if a Dutch breeder, Ms E van Vliet had not imported them here when she moved to Britain in the early 1980's. Dave Cannon took on some of the van Vliet stock and worked with her to produce a British breed standard and gain B.R.C. recognition in 1990.

The early stock in Britain was mainly agouti in colour but it was not long before other breeders in Britain became interested in the breed and imported other colours from Holland so that now all colours recognised by the B.R.C. are accepted. There can be little doubt though that the agouti coloured German Lops have the best agouti undercolour of any agouti coloured rabbit.

Considering the breed was only recognised in Britain in 1990 and the German Lop Club was not formed until the 90's it is quite remarkable that Mr and Mrs Powell won the London Championship Show with a red eyed white German Lop in 1998 and that since then the breed's popularity has increased to the point where they are the third most popular lop (behind the Miniature and the Dwarf Lop) to be exhibited at the Bradford Championship Show and are consistent winners at Open Shows throughout the country.

Special Care

It would be very easy to say that no special care is required to keep German Lops for the breed are renowned for their calm, good nature; they are not unduly large or heavy, are excellent mothers raising large litters of healthy babies and make equally excellent exhibition or pet rabbits.

However, like the French Lop they do have a very ample undercoat with a dense coat that is slightly longer than the coat of the other lops. This can certainly create problems at moult time. Many German Lop breeders either keep their stock in outdoor hutches or in a semi-outdoor situation that provides cover for the breeder attending his stock yet allows the lops to be exposed to the elements.

Because of the logistics of caring for a large number of rabbits most breeders keep their stock in some form of 'shed' but the enclosed environment that the shed creates is not conducive to dense, longish coated lops and therefore they are better to be housed outside, even if it is only during the moult season, to aid the rapid clearing of the coat.

Perhaps because the German Lop has such a pleasant nature they can very easily be overfed. Whilst this could create obvious problems for the exhibition German Lop keeper that must keep their lops within the disqualification weight of 8½lb it can also be the cause of a variety of problems for the pet German Lop owner.

Overweight lops have difficulty grooming and cleaning themselves and are therefore susceptible to fly strike; overweight does are much less likely to carry live babies and are generally more likely to fall prey to all manner of diseases. It must therefore be a priority of German Lop keepers and breeders to keep their lops lean and fit and not to fall for their wonderful disposition and overfeed them.

As the German Lops are such good breeders and raise large healthy litters, anyone breeding them should make sure that they have a suitable outlet for their surplus stock.

There can be no truer saying than 'you cannot keep everything you breed' and this saying is certainly pertinent to the breeder of German Lops. Although the German Lop has gained in popularity in recent years they are unlikely to be as popular as the Miniature Lop, therefore the breeder of German Lops must ensure that there is a local market for their surplus before they start breeding.

Showing

The German Lop has risen in popularity on the show bench in recent years and this really is no surprise as the quality lops have spread from the hands of a few dedicated breeder across the country. There are now many studs breeding superb type into their German Lops and when this type is combined with the very good colour that many German Lops carry then it is little wonder that they are winning at Open Shows across the country almost every week of the year.

Unlike the other flat-faced lops the German Lops rarely suffer from poor ear carriage; because of the weight of the broad and comparatively short ears (11-12 inches from tip to tip, including the skull) and the highly developed crown the German Lop's ears rarely remain erect.

With the ear carriage problem rarely seen breeders can concentrate on type and colour and there certainly are many excellent examples of the breed being exhibited these days. This general high standard means that anyone coming new to the breed will have to attain a very high standard if they are to compete with the established breeders.

Whilst there are a few coloured exhibits with dark feet i.e. the blacks, blues and sooty fawns the majority of the popular colours of German Lops being exhibited have white or light feet. This means that the German Lop exhibitor must perfect the art of keeping their show lops clean so that they can be presented to the judge in immaculate condition.

Whilst there are numerous ways of cleaning white or light

coloured feet, and every exhibitor has their own secret method, there can be no doubt that the easiest way is to prevent them getting dirty in the first place. This can be easier said than done, but the novice exhibitor must adapt their maintenance regime to achieve this standard of cleanliness in their exhibition stock.

Because it is generally only bucks that are shown as adults and because bucks are generally cleaner than does, then with a little ingenuity and some extra work the show buck can be kept clean.

Show bucks should be kept on wood shavings to prevent them getting sore hocks, therefore it is imperative that a regular supply of 'white' shavings that do not contain colourings or dyes is found.

If the hutch is thoroughly cleaned out on a regular basis, say once a week, then all that is required to prevent those white feet getting stained is to add a thin layer of fresh shavings each day and to remove the toilet corner every two or three days.

The keeper of exhibition lops with white or light coloured feet will have a far easier and more rewarding life if the lop's feet are not allowed to get stained in the first place.

German Lop Breed Standard

Ring Size L   Points

1, Overall Type and Shape	30
2. Head and Crown	20
3. Ears	20
4. Coat	15
5. Colour and Pattern	10
6. Condition	5
Total	100

1.Type – Very cobby, massive and muscular. The neck on a good German Lop should not be visible. Ideally it should be equally as broad in the shoulder as in the hind quarters. From the short nape the line of the back should rise in a slight curve to a well-muscled rump which should be short and well rounded. The front legs are short, straight and thick. The hind legs should lie parallel to the rump and not jutting out when resting. A dewlap in does is permissible.

2. Head – The head should be strongly developed with a distinct width between the eyes. The German Lop should have a Roman nose appearance with well-developed cheeks.

3. Ears – The ears should be broad, thick and of good substance, they rise from a strong ridge called a crown on top of the head, carried closely to the cheeks, with openings turned inwards. The ears should hang down straight just behind the eyes without either being carried forwards or backwards. Ear length, measured across the skull minimum 27.96cms – maximum 35.5cms (11-14ins. maximum).

4. Coat – The fur is of normal length, very dense with strong guard hairs.

5. Colour or Pattern – All recognised colours are accepted as well as the butterfly pattern.

6. **Condition.**

Desired Weight – Adult, minimum 2.948kgs – maximum 3,855kgs (6½ – max 8½lbs).

Disqualifications – Weight over 3.855kgs (8½lbs). Putty nose on Butterfly pattern. White patches on coloured rabbits.

Interpretation of the Standard

With 30 points for overall type and shape added to 20 for head and crown and another 20 on ears it can readily be seen that a great deal of emphasis is placed on the shape of the German Lop.

The cobby, massive, muscular type packed into a short powerful body is an absolute must for the exhibition German Lop and any German Lop that does not display these qualities should not even be considered as a show rabbit.

When judging a German Lop for its suitability for exhibition the lop should be placed on a low table facing you so that you are looking down on it. From this angle you will be able to see its body shape which should be as broad in the shoulder as it is in the hindquarters; it is these massive shoulders that not only give the German Lop its characteristic shape but also make the difference between exhibition and pet German Lops, for it is only these specimens that have the massive shoulders that will also have no visible neck.

Having observed the lop from above it should then be viewed from the side where the line of the back should rise in a slight curve to the short, well rounded, well muscled rump.

If the German Lop displays these characteristics then you should stand in front of it with it facing you, then place one hand on the rump applying only slight pressure to keep it down, and with your other hand grasping the base of the ears slightly raise the lop's head so that you can observe the front legs.

The feet should remain just touching the table, but with the weight taken off the head and shoulders and the backend held down you will get the ideal view of the front legs that should be short, straight and strong.

Although not shown in the breed standard as a fault many Judges will penalise an agouti coloured lop that has 'barred' i.e. stripes of a different colour on the front legs. This may seem slightly unfair but the agouti German Lop that is going to win at the highest level will not have barred front feet.

Many people, and indeed many books, state that the German Lop is the same as a French Lop but just a bit smaller. It is the shape of the head of the German Lop that tells the real truth – that the German Lop is not just a small French Lop. The German Lop should have a Roman nose and as it should also have a distinct width between the eyes and well-developed cheeks the Roman nose can only be seen when the lop is viewed in side profile.

There are German Lops around that have been crossed with French Lops to improve the massiveness of the body and shoulders and it is in these crossed rabbits that the flat face of the French Lop is often seen rather than the distinct Roman 'bent' nose that the German Lop requires. The breeder that tries to gain the extra edge by breeding a French Lop into a line of German Lops will be caught out on this feature that really separates the breeds.

The ears are well described in the Breed Standard and so long as the standard is interpreted fully then there can be little ambiguity. With only 15 points for coat and guard hairs one may, wrongly, assume that little importance is attached to the coat.

When it comes to winning in the Challenges no rabbit, no matter how good its type is, will succeed if it does not have a good coat. So whilst the Breed Standard may put little emphasis on coat, if a German Lop excels type then it must be presented with an excellent coat if it is to do itself justice.

If we add the 15 for coat to the 10 points for colour and 5 points for condition then we can see in fact there are a total of 30 points for coat, colour and condition. So quite rightly it is the complete package that is required if a German Lop is to win. However, if it does not have that all important body and type then it will never win, no matter how good its coat, colour and condition.

Because of its size it is unlikely that the German Lop will ever be as popular as its little cousin, the Miniature Lop; it certainly has gained in popularity in recent years and it is not unimaginable that it may overtake the Dwarf Lop in popularity.

A few dedicated breeders have ensured that the standard of the best German Lops is indeed very high and these breeders consistently take the top honours in Open Shows throughout the country.

If this trend continues then there can be little doubt that this powerhouse of a lop will attract even more followers who will win even more shows with them. Although the German Lop has not spread widely across the globe it would appear that its future is certainly safe in Britain.

Chapter 12
The Meissner Lop

Meissner Lop. Exhibitor Wern Stud

History

With the English Lop known to have been bred for exhibition for almost two hundred years and the French Lop since 1853 (albeit in France and Germany) it may come as somewhat of a surprise to many to find that the Meissner Lop was first exhibited at Leipzig in 1906.

The Meissner Lop was created in Meissen, Germany by Mr Leo Reck at the turn of the last century. Unfortunately for us he kept the formula of this beautiful, but different lop to himself and therefore we can only assume that he used the English Lop, almost certainly the French Lop and the Silver. Some references are made to the use of the Argente de Champagne but this is almost certainly supposition as no one really knows exactly what was used.

The original Meissner Lops only came in one colour – black; whilst we know that Mr Neupold worked on the introduction of different colours in the early part of the twentieth century we are not sure exactly in what order the various colours that are now recognised arrived.

We do know that the Black and the Yellow were around when the breed was first recognised in Holland in 1927. The Meissner Lop is now recognised in the four self colours but they differ slightly from the four colours of the Silver. Two of the colours are given slightly different names, so we have the Black Meissner and the Grey Silver, the Yellow Meissner and the Fawn Silver and then the Blue and the Brown. In Germany they also recognise the Havana Meissner.

In Britain the Meissner Lop is looked after by the Rare Varieties Club which is not surprising as it is virtually unknown by the general public and indeed rarely seen on the show bench except for major Championship Shows where the dedicated few who keep the breed always ensure that it is represented.

In Britain the Meissner Lop has never been in the hands of any more than a couple of breeders and whilst over the years many have been attracted to the breed and dabbled with it (this author included) if it had not been for those dedicated followers that have stuck by the breed then it is almost certain that it would have disappeared from our shores and the Fancy would be the poorer for it.

Special Care

The Meissner Lop is a very undemanding rabbit and requires little special attention. Because of the length and density of its coat it is probably best kept in the cooler parts of the country and then either in very well ventilated sheds or outdoors as too much heat can cause them to live in a semi-permanent state of moult.

Meissner Lops are generally calm and affectionately natured

rabbits; the does are excellent mothers making large well-furred nests, giving birth to large, generally healthy litters and producing ample milk to raise them on.

The kits are self coloured when young and do not start to gain their distinctive silvering until about six weeks of age and often do not silver completely until they attain their adult coat at six to eight months of age.

The Meissner Lop is a large rabbit, up to 12 pounds 2 ounces in weight, and should therefore be housed in a suitably large hutch to enable it to exercise sufficiently. As with the other large lops it should be bedded on a deep layer of shavings covered with barley straw to prevent sore hocks developing.

Showing

Because of the paucity of Meissner Lops in Britain most judges rarely have the opportunity to judge them, which means that they have to rely on the written Breed Standard and have little experience to compare them with. Only those judges that frequently judge in the areas where the few dedicated breeders live really see the Meissners often enough to have any experience of the breed.

Perhaps the most common error of judges and stewards alike is to pose the Meissner Lop 'coupled' in, that is to say with the rear end of the rabbit tucked in as you would do for all the other lops except the English Lop. If the Meissner is posed incorrectly in this way it gives it the appearance of being a much shorter rabbit than it actually is. The body is described in the Breed Standard as being 'slightly longish' and it is this important look that can be completely ruined by those inexperienced in handling the breed. The rabbit should be allowed to sit naturally and comfortably so that it can show off the full length of its body.

If the Meissner Lop is handled correctly on the table it should cause few problems, for like the other big lops it is usually quite placid and readily adapts to the rigours of show life.

Because the Meissner Lop is a large lop it should be bedded on a deep layer of shavings with added barley straw when in a show pen. This will make the animal more relaxed as it is being kept in the same manner as it is at home and prevent a rough join in the floor of the pen causing damage to the hocks that could well take many months to repair.

It is difficult to show young (under five month old) Meissner Lops as they do not fully 'silver' until they are in adult coat and as the judge is likely to refer to the standard that says 'top coat should be evenly silvered over the whole body' he will almost certainly see the lack of silvering, particularly on the ears and legs on a young Meissner, as a fault.

As was stated earlier the Meissner Lop's coat does not cope well with the heat and they can be quite difficult to get into full coat. The fully grown adult that is completely and evenly silvered and is in full coat is indeed a magnificent lop but unfortunately rarely seen, for they tend to only hold that 'full coat' for such a short period of time.

Meissner Lop Breed Standard

Ring Size H	Points
1. Type	20
2. Head and Ears	15
3. Weight	20
4. Fur	15
5. Colour – Top Colour	15
Under Colour	10
6. Condition	5
Total	100

1. Type – Not so massive as the French Lop – resembles the English Lop in type of head. Body slightly longish. Back nicely curved (not mandolin type) with well-rounded rump. Wide rump and chest. Legs thick and strong. No dewlap on buck, small one allowed on doe.

2. Head and Ears – Head has a distinct bent (Roman look) but not French Lop type of face. Strong head with wide forehead, finer in doe. Ears are well set, tube-like at base and carried full. Inside aspect of ears facing the cheeks. Length of ears 38-42cm (15-16 ins.).

3. Weight – 3.5 – 5.5 kgs (7lb 12ozs – 12lb 2ozs).

4. Fur – Very dense with good even ticking, length 2.54 – 3.81 cms (1-11½ ins).

5. Colours – recognised are black, blue, brown and yellow and the topcoat should be evenly silvered over the whole body with a rich sheen, under colour to match body colour as closely as possible.

6. Condition – as standard for all breeds.

Interpretation of the Breed Standard

The Meissner Lop Breed Standard is indeed quite odd as the British Standard was altered in 2001 to change the weight limits from 7lbs(3.17kgs) - 9lbs(4.07kgs) to 7lbs 12oz (3.5kgs) – 12lbs 2 oz (5.5kgs). These massive changes to the British Breed Standard brought it into line with the German standard, leaving only the Dutch standard still having an upper weight limit of 10lbs (4.5kgs).

The result of this change is that overnight the upper weight limit for a Meissner Lop being judged under B.R.C. rules changed by 3lbs 2ozs. However, it was a change that was to have important implications for British breeders as it allowed for the all-important importation of new blood from Germany, something that was not possible when they were breeding much bigger rabbits than ours.

The wide weight allowance (7lbs12ozs-12lbs2ozs) in the British Breed Standard has thrown up a curious anomaly, for there are 20 points allocated to weight but no guide lines whatsoever as to what is an ideal weight. One must therefore ask: how does the judge allocate those 20 points? This anomaly is compounded when you consider there are 20 points for type and only 15 points for the head and ears and yet this undefined weight is given equal importance. It is little wonder that judges rarely place a Meissner Lop high in the Challenges when in fact the judge could never really give an exhibit a score of more than 80 points.

Having discussed what the judge cannot actually score let us now look at what he can give some points for. Although we may have the weight up to 12lbs 2ozs which is almost certainly bigger than most English Lops being exhibited today, and in fact bigger than many of the French Lops that are seen on the table, the Meissner is described as 'not so massive as the French Lop' so where does it carry that considerable weight? As we have already said the body is 'slightly longish' and it is this slightly longish body that must have a wide rump and chest and thick strong legs – not much of a description for a judge to allocate his 20 points on.

The notes in the standard do say that the back of the Meissner Lop should be 'nicely curved (not mandolin type)'. Exactly what the definition of 'nicely' is, one is left wondering, although the reference to the mandolin shape is a clear hint that the Meissner Lop should not be shown 'coupled in', an act that will certainly enhance the back end and could well give it a mandolin appearance. Also, that it should not look like the English Lop which of course should have a mandolin shape.

The notes on the allocation of the 15 points awarded for the head and ears are similarly vague. Whilst we are told that the Meissner Lop should have a 'distinct bent' (Roman look) but not French Lop type of face' perhaps what we should have been told is that the Meissner Lop should have a 'distinct bent (Roman look) but not English Lop type face'. For the English Lop also has a Roman nose but it is very different to that of the Meissner Lop, whereas the French Lop is flat faced and therefore has no resemblance whatsoever to the look required of the Meissner Lop.

We are not told in the British Breed Standard if the Meissner should or should not have a 'crown'. The German standard does state that the Meissner Lop should (unlike the English Lop) have a crown. So although the ears are quite well described (not as well as in the German standard) one is left wondering just how most judges would go about allocating the 15 points allowed for the head and ears.

The Meissner Lop should have a very dense coat throughout and the 15 points allocated for coat will obviously be rolled in with the 5 points for condition in the judge's mind so that this dense coat should be in good condition and not showing any signs of moult.

In the notes on colour we are offered the advice that 'the topcoat should be evenly silvered over the whole body with a rich sheen' but we are given no description of the colour required.

Bearing in mind the resemblance to the Silver rabbit we should have been offered something along the lines of 'top coat to resemble the equivalent Silver in colour' or given a description of each colour.

Similarly we are told in the Meissner Lop Breed Standard notes that the 'undercolour to match body colour as closely as possible' but as we are not given a description of the body colour one wonders how a Judge is to make this comparison.

It will also be noted if one studies the Breed Standard for the Silver that in fact the Silver Grey that has a 'rich black' top colour has a blue-black undercolour. We cannot compare the Silver Brown with the Brown Meissner as the Silver is an agouti whereas the Brown Meissner is a self.

The top colour is allocated a total of 15 points and this includes the all important silvering. This is described simply as 'the topcoat should be evenly silvered over the whole body with a rich sheen' so most judges would automatically want to put great emphasis on the silvering and its presence or absence on the head, ears and legs. With so few points and such a thin description of what is required then it really is little wonder any two judges assessing the same Meissner Lop on the same day would almost certainly differ widely in their allocation of the points.

When one compares the Meissner Lop Breed Standard with that of say, the Miniature Lop it is little wonder that the Meissner rarely does well in Open Shows. Any judge assessing a quality Miniature Lop has such a detailed description of what is required that the rabbit has every chance of scoring a very high total out of the 100 available points but sadly this is not the case for the Meissner Lop for as hard as a judge may try, using the present Breed Standard, it would be extremely difficult for him to allocate anything resembling a high score.

Perhaps if a new, detailed Meissner Lop Breed Standard were to be submitted for publication in the next B.R.C. Breed Standards Book then those dedicated breeders who have stuck with this delightful breed over the years would start to see some recognition for all their hard work in the Lop Challenges.

Chapter 13
The Miniature Lop

Chinchilla. (Fur & Feather picture library)

Black Otter. Exhibited by Mr & Mrs Evans

Black. (Fur & Feather picture library)

White. Exhibited by Mr & Mrs Evans

Blue. Exhibited by Cheryl Faint

Sooty Fawn. Exhibited by Foxley Stud

Agouti. Exhibited by Cheryl Faint

Blue Otter. Exhibited by Darren Morris

Sable. (Fur & Feather picture library)

Agouti Butterfly. (Fur & Feather picture library)

History

The Miniature Lop breed standard was accepted by the British Rabbit Council in November 1994 and the National Miniature Lop Rabbit Club was formally granted affiliation at a meeting of the B.R.C. Management Committee on January 28th 1995. Looking back now this could be seen as the start of the Miniature Lop in Britain, but nothing could be further from the truth; a few dedicated fanciers had already put many years of hard work into the development of this delightful little lop.

In the months prior to November 1994 and the Miniature Lop standard being accepted, the late John Sandford did much work bringing two clubs and two standards together.

In the early 1990's a number of British fanciers, amongst them

Hilary Cannon and Phyllis Chell, imported 'Nederlandse Hangoor Dwerg' rabbits from Holland. These small lops, that had been reduced in size by the Dutch, soon found their way into the hands of a group of dedicated breeders in Britain. They formed the Holland Lop Club, which was not affiliated to the B.R.C., to co-ordinate efforts to develop the breed in Britain. All the imported rabbits were ear tattooed by their breeders prior to importation into Britain.

At about the same time, the British Mini Lop Club, again an unaffiliated organisation, was formed to promote the breeding of a small lop eared rabbit using British blood lines that had been developed from Dwarf Lops.

These British blood lines had evolved from stock that had originally been imported into Britain in the late 1960's by Mike Guy and Gwenda Tose and shortly afterwards by George Scott and Meg Brown. The imported stock had been created by Adriann Van de Cock of Tilburg, Holland in 1964, using small French Lops, Netherland Dwarfs, Dutch and English Lops.

Shortly after this a Ministry ban prevented further importation to Britain. In a further twist to the story a business man, Angio Chiesa who frequented Europe a great deal, imported ten more little lops in 1978. Smaller animals than the Scott/Brown ones, they had to spend six months in quarantine and some did not survive.

It should be pointed out that the lops that were being imported into, and subsequently bred in, Britain were generally in the 4 - 5 lb weight range. Cheisa showed his lops at the Adult Stock Show at Coventry in 1979 and won overall Best in Show with a sooty fawn. There was a huge demand for the offspring from Cheisa's stock and it is from this stock that the Dwarf Lop was developed.

It was found that when this early stock was bred for shortness of body it often did not make the weight required for the Dwarf Lop and these smaller animals were then used to keep the larger ones inside the upper weight limit (5¼ lb). It did not take long before some fanciers realised that these smaller Cheisa lops could be worked on to become the Mini Lop.

Perhaps most notable for their work on the British 'mini lop' during the late 1980's and early 1990's were Tony Rice, the well known Tan breeder, and Jane Bramley.

Unfortunately Tony Rice died in 1993 and therefore did not live to see his dream of the B.R.C. accepting a standard for the Mini Lop come true.

However, prior to Tony's death Peter Faint of Cumbria had shown an interest and actually acquired some of Tony's stock. So it was that Jane Bramley and Peter Faint took the British Mini Lop forward to the point in 1994 where they applied to the Management Committee of the B.R.C. for the standard to be accepted and to affiliate the British Mini Lop Club to the B.R.C.

Peter Faint's Agouti "British Mini Lop" shown at Bacup Championship Show in June 1993

However, they were refused because about the same time the Holland Lop Club, with their imported rabbits, were applying for their standard to be accepted and for their club to be affiliated to the B.R.C.

The Management Committee felt that the two 'types' of small lop were so similar that the Breed Standards Committee should work with both sets of breeders to produce a standard that would be

acceptable to both groups. The amalgamation of the two clubs into a new club to be known as the National Miniature Lop Rabbit Club, the constitution, and the new Standard were agreed in principle and the new rings (size K) were issued in November 1994.

Solo Morris Minor: best in show success at the 1999 London Championship Show

The first meeting of the new Committee was held at the 1995 Bradford Championship show. To return to the beginning of this brief history of the Club, it was formally granted affiliation at a meeting of the Management Committee on the 28th January 1995.

A close inspection of the Miniature Lops at a major Championship show will still identify the two different sources of foundation stock, for there is quite a difference in them; the Holland lop stock has a smaller 'apple shaped' head and tends to sit 'higher', whereas the scaled down dwarf lop stock is often described as brick shaped and usually has a much larger head.

As to which 'type' is favoured by the judges it is hard to say, certainly Peter Faint with his scaled down dwarf lop type was the major force in the first five years of Club Stock shows.

However, whilst both types of Miniature Lop are now consistent winners in Open shows there has only been one major

Championship Show win by a Miniature Lop and that was the Holland lop type agouti, Solo Morris Minor, bred by Susan Carlisle (now Lyons) at London in 1999.

Special Care

The Miniature Lop is a very tame little lop that can often be quite mischievous and inquisitive. The does are generally good mothers but can be protective of their young. Some have poor conception rates, with litter sizes usually between 2 and 4. The litter may well contain one or even two 'peanuts', these tiny babies have inherited a double dwarfing gene and are extremely unlikely to survive.

Although the kits are best left with the mother until 8 to 10 weeks of age the mother may well not tolerate them for that length of time and they may well have to be separated earlier.

Malocclusion and body size are the two main problems in the Miniature Lop; breeders must be prepared to carry out strict culling to eliminate both of these faults.

Pat Duffy, Chairman of the National Miniature Lop Rabbit Club carried out some very useful research in the early days of the Club that resulted in the publication of a weight by age graph. Whilst it is

emphasised in the accompanying article that animals like humans may vary and that the graph cannot be taken as gospel for every young Miniature Lop, it is a rough guide and any youngster that deviates too much from the norm will almost certainly not mature into a lop of acceptable weight.

Age (in months)

0	1	2	3	4	5	6	7	8	9	10
3oz	14oz	1lb 6oz	1lb 14oz	2lb 5oz	2lb 10oz	2lb 14oz	3lb 1oz	3lb 3oz	3lb 4oz	3lb 4oz

Weight (in pounds and ounces)

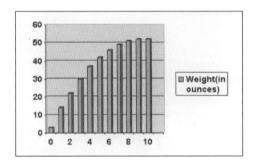

Age in months

Whilst a Miniature Lop should conform roughly to this graph it cannot be stressed strongly enough that the first few months of a lop's life are vital for its development. The starving of a lop to keep it following the pattern of the graph should not be attempted under any circumstances whatsoever.

If a lop is clearly going to be outside the requirements for a show rabbit then it can be sold as a pet and therefore removed from the breeding programme. Many breeders are in fact happy to keep large does that are to be used for breeding believing them to carry larger and healthier litters; however, an oversize buck is of no use for show or breeding.

Showing

Since it was first accepted by the B.R.C. in 1995 the Miniature Lop has proved to be a very popular show rabbit. Nowhere is this more clearly seen than in the entry figures for the Bradford Championship show. At the 1996 event 67 Miniature Lops were exhibited; by 2000 the Miniature Lop had surpassed the Dwarf Lop becoming the most popular lop exhibited, and the entry figure rose to 112 in 2001. It has since levelled off (110 - 2002 and 112 - 2003). The Miniature Lop now stands as the third most popular rabbit, and most popular lop rabbit exhibited at the Bradford Championship show.

It was the Miniature Lop breeders and exhibitors who were the driving force behind the successful 2001 bid to get a separate Lop Diploma at all B.R.C. supported shows.

Whilst there are still some areas in Britain where few Miniature Lops are found, they are now well represented throughout most areas of the country.

The Miniature Lop is a very easy rabbit to show; it adapts very quickly to the rigours of show life and it requires little or no special attention. Of course they must be presented fit and in immaculate condition just like any other rabbit that an exhibitor hopes to win with. If they have been trained to behave and present themselves correctly on the show table then there are few rabbits to beat them.

Weight still remains the biggest obstacle to the success of the Miniature Lop. The ideal weight is 3lb 4oz but an overweight lop that has been starved to get within the weight limit of 3lb 8oz will invariably, and quite rightly, be penalised by judges as the loss of condition and flesh along the back and hips is all too easy to spot.

Conversely the very small Miniature Lop of below 3lb is unlikely to do well in the adult classes at it will lack the boldness called for in the standard.

All exhibitors of Miniature Lops should be aware that the members of the National Miniature Lop Rabbit Club voted to introduce a maximum weight of 3 pounds for under five month exhibits.

This rule was introduced to stop breeders breeding large Miniature Lops that will almost certainly go over weight as adults.

Miniature Lop Breed Standard

Ring Size K	Points	
1. Type	)	30
2. Weight	)	
3. Coat		20
4. Head, Crown and Eyes	)	
5. Ears	)	30
6. Colour and Pattern		15
7. Condition		5
	Total	100

1. **Type** – Bold, thickset and firm. The body should be short, broad and well muscled with little visible neck. The well-muscled rump is short and well rounded. The chest is broad and deep with curved sides where it meets the shoulders, which are broad and strong; the front legs are thick, short and straight. The hind legs are short, strong, and powerful and carried parallel to the body. The tail is straight, strong and well-furred. A small dewlap is permissible but not desirable.

2. **Weight** – Ideal 1.5kg (3lb 4ozs), Maximum 1.6kg(3lb 8oz), maximum weight for under 5 months exhibits to be 1.360kg(3lb).

3. **Coat** – The coat to be dense and of good length, rollback with an abundance of guard hairs. Legs and pads to be well furred.

4. **Head, Crown and Eyes** – The head is bold, broad and well developed. The profile of the head is strongly curved with a good width between the eyes, full cheeks and a broad muzzle. The eyes are bold, bright and large. The basal ridge of the ears should appear prominent across the top of the skull to form the crown.

5. **Ears** – Should be broad, thick, well furred and rounded at the ends. They should be carried close to the cheeks giving a horseshoe like outline when viewed from the front. The inside of the ears should not be visible from any angle when carried correctly.

6. **Colour and Pattern** – Any colour or pattern accepted by the

Breeds Standard Committee of the British Rabbit Council.

7. **Condition** – The exhibit should be in a perfect state of health and bodily condition, free from all soiling, particularly on the feet, ears and genital parts. The coat should reflect the overall good health of the exhibit, which should appear alert and vigorous.

Faults: Body too long; head not sufficiently characteristic of the breed; pimpled or damaged ears; poor ear carriage; ears folded; crown not developed; fly back coat, large dewlap in does; rear feet not parallel to the body; slight soiling of feet; ears and genital organs; bare pads; fur slightly soiled or matted; long toenails; lack of vitality.

Disqualifications: Maloccluded or mutilated teeth; over weight limit; deformities and mutilations; deformation of the teeth; ears tipped over, feet bowed or bent; white toe nails in coloured exhibits; crooked tail; any discernible illness or disease; blindness or partial blindness; incorrect eye colour; any parasitic infection; much soiling; matted coat; sore pads (where skin is broken or scabbed); any evidence of irregular preparation for exhibition including trimming or dyeing.

Interpretation of the Standard

The Miniature Lop standard is perhaps the most detailed of all the lop standards and it is in the 'Faults' and 'Disqualifications' that the real detail is to be found. In fact the biggest failing of most Miniature Lops is encompassed in the very first line of the Faults - body too long, head not sufficiently characteristic of the breed. There are still some poor quality Miniature Lops being exhibited at the smaller shows, being long in the body and narrow in the head. These type of lops must be eradicated from the breed, but all the judges can do is penalise them as a fault.

With a total of 60 points on type, weight, head, crown and eye much emphasis is rightly given to the type and structure of the rabbit and it must be said that in the relatively short history of the Miniature Lop they have improved out of all recognition.

For a long time the only quality Miniature Lops were in the hands of a few, however, in recent years those quality lops have found their way into the hands of many and the general standard throughout the country is now much improved. The all important short body and broad, bold head are goals that every breeder of Miniature Lops has long aspired to, but now that this type is spreading throughout the country the next challenge must be to work on improving colour.

With 15 points for colour and pattern the Miniature Lop breeders' next challenge must be to stop mixing their colours and breed only like to like, so that quality of the colour can be improved.

Because the Dutch used the Netherland Dwarf in the development of the Miniature Lop the breed is lucky in that it has a great diversity of colours. However, many are shown that would fail colour in other breeds and the standard does say that 'any colour or pattern accepted by the Breeds Standards Committee of the British Rabbit Council' which means that the colour or pattern must be as good as in any other breed.

Oranges with black guard hairs, agoutis lacking banding or having grey sides and black otters with silver ticking are but just three examples of major colour/pattern failures that are seen all too often in Miniature Lops. If the same dedication is applied in the next few years to colour as has been applied to improving type then we should start to see the more complete package in the not too distant future.

If breeders can bring about a general improvement in colour then with it should come an improvement in coat; with 20 points allocated in the standard for coat this would undoubtedly be good for the breed.

The standard requires the coat to be 'dense and of good length' and to have 'rollback with an abundance of guard hairs'. This can only be achieved by true colour breeding so that the correct mix of guard hairs and undercoat can be bred into the lops. A coat with too few guard hairs will always appear dead and thus never have 'rollback', whereas, a coat with too many guard hairs will fly back. Fly back is listed as a fault in the Miniature Lop's coat and will be penalised by the judge.

Considering the very short period of time that the quality Miniature Lops have been in the hands of the masses the type has undoubtedly improved beyond all recognition but there is still work to be done to eradicate those long narrow animals that are being bred by a few. A lot of work on breeding true colours will bring about an improvement in coat quality.

With its wonderful temperament, mischievous nature and increasing popularity amongst Fanciers there can be little doubt that the future of the Miniature Lop is in good hands and that many of the major shows will be won by Minis as yet unborn.

Under five months Black buck exhibited by Ridgerose Stud. Photo: Richard Chaff

Chapter 14
The Miniature Cashmere Lop

Miniature Cashmere RE White. Exhibited by Kalian Stud

Miniature Cashmere Sooty Fawn. Exhibited by Sally Ann Murphy

History

The Miniature Cashmere Lop is the newest member of the lop family; the very first one to be exhibited at the Bradford Championship Show was shown there in 2001. However, just like the introduction of so many of the other lop breeds the acceptance and first showing at the Bradford Championship Show is in fact the culmination of many years of work by a small band of dedicated fanciers.

Just like its bigger relation the Cashmere Lop, the Miniature Cashmere Lop probably first appeared as a long-haired genetic mutation in litters of the smaller Dwarf Lops that were being developed in the early 1980's.

In fact the first one to be shown to the Fancy was a little Black Fox buck in 1982. But acceptance was slow and it was not until the late 1980's that Jane Bramley bred the first 'litter' of Miniature Cashmere Lops.

The Miniature Cashmere Lop was in the early 1990's to suffer from the rapidly rising popularity of the Miniature Lop. As breeders across the country worked to reduce the Cheisa lops to produce the Mini Lop and others imported the Holland Lop (see Chapter 13), two events that culminated in the acceptance and subsequent meteoric rise in popularity of the Miniature Lop, so the development of the Miniature Cashmere Lop took a back seat.

Once the Miniature Lop had gained acceptance and settled to its new found popularity then the admirers of the cashmere variant could turn their full attention to the breed and start the lengthy process of gaining the B.R.C's acceptance of the breed standard.

This acceptance of the Breed Standard for the Miniature Cashmere Lop was achieved in 2000 for a limited number of colours and the breed was taken under the wing of the National Cashmere Lop Club. The breed now has full acceptance and is regularly seen in Open Shows across the country and no doubt it will not be too many years before we see this delightful little lop gaining the top honours at major shows.

Special Care

As the Miniature Cashmere Lop is a Miniature Lop with a

Cashmere Coat then the special care required for a Cashmere Lop (see Chapter 7 – The Cashmere Lop) should be applied as should the special care for the Miniature Lop (see Chapter 13 – The Miniature Lop).

Showing

The cashmere coat of the Miniature Cashmere Lop dictates that the notes on Showing for the Cashmere Lop (see Chapter 7) are equally applicable for the Miniature Cashmere Lop.

The Miniature Cashmere Lop Breed Standard

Ring size C	Points
1. Type and Condition	30
2. Head, Ears and Crown	30
3. Coat	30
4. Colour	10
Total	100

1.Type – Bold thickset and firm. The body should be short, broad and well muscled with little visible neck. The well muscled rump is short and well rounded. The chest is broad and deep. The overall appearance giving a compact impression. The front legs are thick short and straight. The hind legs are short, strong and powerful and carried parallel to the body. The tail is strong, straight and well furred.

2.Head, Ears and Crown – The head should be strong, bold and broad with well developed cheeks set well into the shoulders. The ears are broad, thick, well furred and rounded at the ends, they are carried close to the cheeks, giving a horseshoe like shape when viewed from the front. The inside of the ears should not be visible from any angle when carried correctly. The crown, which is the basal ridge of each ear, should be prominent across the top of the skull. The eyes should be bold and bright.

3.Coat – Fur is dense, the topcoat being longer and heavier than the under-coat with plenty of longer, stronger guard hairs.

Approximately 1 ½ ins – 2ins long the coat should not be woolly, matted or felted, to hang down naturally. Evenness is more important than length.

4.Colour – After the initial acceptance of only four colours for the Miniature Cashmere Lop the standard has now been brought into line with all the other Lop Breed Standards and 'all recognised colours and patterns' are now accepted.

Weight – 1.6kg (3lbs 8oz) maximum.

Faults – White hairs in solid colours. White toe nails in coloured exhibits. Putty noses in Butterfly pattern. Coats with extremes of softness or harshness.

Disqualification – Overweight, waviness in coat, malocclusion, any deformities.

Interpretation of the Breed Standard

Now that the full range of colours has been accepted for the breed it is only the weight limitation of the Miniature Cashmere Lop that differentiate the Breed Standard from that of the Cashmere Lop (see Chapter 7).

Chapter 15
Colour and Pattern

Part 1 The Colours

In all the Lop Breed Standards except the Meissner Lop[1] the standard has a statement to the effect "Any other colour or pattern[2] that conforms to the colour or pattern of recognised breeds". In other words, if a colour or pattern has been accepted by the Breeds Standards Committee of the British Rabbit Council then it is acceptable in a Lop.

It is somewhat surprising, therefore that there is no comprehensive document that lists and describes all the colours and patterns in one place for easy reference.

True, the British Rabbit Council "Breed Standards" does have a description of the requirements of most of the recognised colours but they are scattered throughout the book with some colours described on numerous occasions whilst others may be found only once if you look long and hard enough.

For completeness all recognised colours and patterns are described as fully as possible

The Chocolate Tortoiseshell Miniature Lop was introduced in January 2002

here for two reasons: firstly to give every exhibitor, new and old, an easily accessible reference and secondly, to inspire those so inclined to look at what could be possible to achieve should they wish to take up the challenge.

There is a paucity of colour variation in the Lops when compared to the Netherland Dwarf which was only recognised as a breed in Great Britain in the 1950's and yet over the last 50 years Nethie fanciers have dedicated much time and skill into the development of new colours.

It would appear that the Miniature Lop could follow the trend set by the Netherland Dwarf as many mini breeders are now dabbling in colour development. This is not meant to be a derogatory statement as there are a few dedicated mini breeders working very hard to recognise new colours, but too many minis are appearing on the show bench that are the result of crossing colours and not to true breeding. It is therefore hoped that the descriptions that follow will encourage both true to true breeding and thus the exhibiting of far better coloured lops, and also, the dedicated to experiment on colour development in their sheds.

The Miniature Lop has 15 points for colour, whereas all the other lops have 10 points, so the perfecting of colour in your stock is well worthwhile so long as type is not compromised. Good colour could just make the difference between success and failure.

Notes:

1. [1]. Meissner only four colours recognised.

2. [2]. The Broken Pattern was recognised in 2001(for the mini rex), however, the NMLRC and the NFDLRC both put forward amendments to their constitutions to ban the broken pattern.

1. Agouti (A.B.C.D.E.)(+r)   ag

A rich chestnut shade with black ticking over an intermediate orange band and a dark slate blue undercolour. Ears laced black. Eye circles, underside of tail and belly to be white with slate undercolour.(in addition the Dwarf Lop standard states ' pale top colour a fault').

Notes – There are six colours in the Agouti Pattern Section

(Agouti, Opal, Lynx, Chinchilla, Squirrel and Cinnamon) and all must have a banded colour in the make up of their coat. When the coat is blown into or parted by hand it should show the following banding:

Starting from the base of the hair at the skin the first band, known as the undercoat or base colour should be dark slate blue with an orange intermediate band and the top colour is a rich chestnut shade interspersed with black ticking. Many agoutis fail some or all of these requirements usually because the agouti is of such good type that it has been used in different colour matings and the resultant agoutis are impure. Two common faults with the agouti are grey sides and barred feet, both of which can be eradicated by careful breeding.

2. Beige (Aa B. C. dd ee)   bei

Dark Chamois or light sandy colour down to the skin, faintly ticked with blue. Hairs tinted light at base, medium in middle and darker at tips. Blue shading on flanks, muzzle, edges of ears. Top sides of hind legs beige, pads blue, forefeet same as body. Tail beige on top, blue under. Belly beige with deeper blue shading.

Notes – Sometimes known as Isabella or Blue Tortoiseshell the Beige is a shaded pattern and as such must exhibit a gradual blend from saddle to flanks, without any patchiness or blotches. The only way to eradicate patchy or blotchiness is to mate to a rabbit that exhibits good shading. It is basically a blue sooty fawn and often shows similar faults to the sooty, light under, light or even white tails.

3. Black (Aa B. C. D. E.)   bk

A deep lustrous solid black carrying well down to the skin with blue or slate blue undercolour. Eyes dark hazel or black.

Notes – Nothing could look more stunning than a full coated black in prime condition, but put half a dozen blacks together on the show bench and you can almost guarantee that you will have half a dozen different shades of black. Blacks must never be left in the sun or they will get a rusty tinge, but more importantly blacks must only be bred to blacks or you will be found out, usually when it matters most. Biggest failings are white undercolour or white hairs, easily cured by breeding true.

4. Bleu and Blue (aa B. C. dd E.)
(Bleu + argente silvering)   bu

Deep or medium slate blue (not lavender) carried well down hair shaft with blue/black undercolour. Eyes dark blue.

Notes – Just like the black, blues suffer from white hairs and white patches, especially in the tail and ear roots and white undercolour. Although difficult to eradicate, breeding with a good pure black can help.

5. Blue-cream (aa B. C. dd ee.)
(long haired equivalent of beige)   buc

Mask and feet blue, wool as for cream but with blue shadings on ears and flanks, with the colour extended across the belly. A blue tinge to the wool and blue tipping is desirable but not essential. Eyes blue-grey.

Notes – This colour is presently only found in the Angora, but could be a challenge for the Cashmere.

6. Blue-grey (A. B. C. dd E.)
(long haired equivalent of opal)   bug

Head, ears and feet a mixture of blue and gold. Wool blue with tips to match head. White belly with blue undercoat. Eyes blue-grey.

Notes – As for 5. Blue-cream.

7. Blue-point (aa B. $c^{chl}c$ dd E.)   bup

Smoky blue on ears, nose (mask) feet and tail. Cream body colour. Eyes to have a distinct ruby glow.

Notes – Brown eyes and too much colour in body are considered faults in this dilute smoke. Too often poor coloured seal-points are passed off as blue-points.

8. Bronze (aa bb C. D. ee)   bz

Rich orange fur dusted with brown, shading gradually on flanks and haunches. Ears, cheeks, face and feet to match rest of shading.

Colour at base of fur may be bluish-white. Eyes brown.

Notes – Only currently found in Satins but basically a brown sooty fawn.

9. Brown and brun (aa bb C. D. E.)
(brun + argente silvering)   bn

A rich dark chocolate, colour going well down the fur with a pearl-grey undercoat.

Notes – Called Chocolate in Lops.

10. Brown-grey (A. B. C. D. E.)(+r)   bng

Slate blue at the base followed by a band of yellowy orange then a black line, finishing by light or nut brown tips to the fur. The whole interspersed with black guard hairs. Eyes hazel, the deeper the better.

Notes – This is basically the Dutch version of the agouti, but note the presence of the black line.

11. Castor (A. B. C. D. E,)(+rr)   ca

Colour to be dark rich chestnut brown. Intermediate colour to be rich orange clearly defined on dark slate blue undercolour. Fur to be lightly tipped with black, chest to match flanks. Head, outside of ears, upperside of tail to match body colour. Ears laced black. Belly and underside of tail white with dark slate undercolour.

Notes – Basically the Fur(Satin) and Rex(Castor) version of Agouti.

12. Champagne (aa B. C. D. E.) (+argente silvering) cm

Undercolour dark slate blue, body colour bluish white, the whole evenly and moderately interspersed with longer, jet black hairs to give old silver effect when viewed from a distance. Eyes brown, toenails horn coloured.

Notes – Only found in the Argente but a beautiful colour.

13. Chinchilla (A. B. c^{chd} D. E.)   ch

Undercolour to be slate blue at base. Intermediate portion pearl with narrow line edging. Pearling to be clearly defined. Top grey brightly ticked with black hairs, neck fur to be lighter in colour than body but strictly confined to nape. Flanks and chest ticked with uniform shade of pearl slightly lighter than body. Eye circles light grey. Ears laced black.

Notes – Although a member of the Agouti family the Chin should not be mated with an Agouti as the chin was derived from the Chinchilla (a Fur rabbit) and has slightly different characteristics. Mating with other members of the agouti family will invariably put a brown tinge on what should be a stunning colour. The only way to improve the colour or banding in a Chin is to mate with a well marked, good coloured one and select carefully.

14. Chinchilla Giganta (A. B. c^{chd} D. E.) (+ dark ticking)   c.gi

As for No.13. Chinchilla but with longer black tipped guard hairs to give a well mixed 'Mackerel' effect. Desired top colour considerably darker than the Chinchilla.

Notes – An unlikely colour to be put into lops but you do occasionally see some poor chin lops with an excess of guard hairs that make you wonder.

15. Cinnamon (A. bb C. D. E.   cin

Colour to be bright golden tan. Intermediate colour to be light orange clearly defined on a blue undercolour. Fur lightly tipped with brown. Chest to match flanks. Head, outside ears, upperside of tail to match body colour. Ears laced brown. Belly and underside to tail white with blue/grey undercolour. Blue and orange bands to be approximately equal in width.

Notes – Another member of the Agouti family. You rarely see Cinnamon lops yet the colour is not a dilute, like the more popular Opals and Lynx and should therefore be easier to put good definition in the banding. The colour is also known as the Chocolate Agouti and the Lynx is a dilute cinnamon.

16. Chocolate (aa bb C. D. E.)   coc

Deep, solid, dark chocolate colour carrying well down to the skin.

Undercolour to match the top colour as near as possible. The deeper the undercolour the better the top colour will appear. Free from white hairs and mealiness. Eyes chocolate or brown.

Notes – Because there are so few Chocolate lops the genetic pool is very small and many of those that are seen seem to lack type. This will undoubtedly improve with the concerted effort of those dedicated individuals who persevere.

16a. Chocolate Tort (aabbC.D.ee)

An even shade of Orange top colour to carry well down and shading off to a lighter colour to the skin. Ears, belly and underside of tail – light chocolate brown. Cheeks and hindquarters (flanks) shaded or toned with light chocolate brown. Eyes brown.

Notes – The latest colour to be accepted by the BRC. The colour was developed on the Miniature Lop and although the colour is accepted much work must now be done to improve the type on the lops of this stunning colour that is in effect a chocolate sooty.

17.   Cream (A.C.dd.ee+rr longhair equivalent of fawn)
cr
Crème (A.C.dd ee+argente silvering)

Undercolour orange to go down as far as possible, body colour creamy white, the whole evenly and moderately interspersed with longer orange hairs to give a distinctly creamy effect when viewed from a distance. White underbelly to be permissible but a coloured underbelly to be encouraged. Eyes bold and dark brown, toenails horn coloured.

Notes – only seen in Argente at present but would make a spectacular lop.

18.   Dark Steel Grey (A.B.C.D.E[s])   dsg

Dark steel grey merging to pale slate blue in the undercolour. The whole is interspersed with black guard hairs. The extreme tips of the fur to be tipped with steel blue or grey. The mixture to carry well down the sides, flanks, hind feet. Belly colour will be a lighter shade varying with top colour, upper part of tail to match body colour, underside to tone with belly colour. Ears to match body. Eyes deep hazel.

Notes – very similar to the steel that is becoming very popular especially in French and Miniature Lops, but this could just be used as an excuse for a poor steel.

19. Deilenaar or Red Agouti(A.B.C.D.E. + rrr)   de

Top Colour & Belly Colour: The top colour is a warm red brown, with strong wavy ticking. This refers to the entire body except the belly and the inside of the hind legs. Muzzle, jawline and inside of ears are tan coloured. The ears are laced with black. The forelegs are heavily ticked, but more regularly ticked than the body because of the shorter fur on them. The ticking on the back, flanks and head should be wavy, to give a 'Mackerel' appearance. The triangle on the nape is rusty red. The colour of the belly is cream to sandy red. There is a thin rusty red line dividing the belly and the body colours. The chest is warm red brown with slight ticking. The eyes are dark brown, nails are dark horn and whiskers are coloured.

Intermediate & Base Colour: The intermediate colour is rusty red brown. The base colour of the body and chest is slate blue and to be evenly divided. The belly undercolour is creamy except at the rust red groin streaks, where the undercolour is blue.

Notes – Spectacular, but may be too much of a challenge, although the Deilenaar is not that far away from the German Lop in type(?). Whilst the Red Agouti Polish may be a similar size to the mini lop it would probably be too much of a challenge to get the type right. However, when one sees a full coated, deep chestnut red Belgian Hare then perhaps putting that georgeous coat onto a lop may well be worthwhile.

20. Fawn (A.C.dd ee)   fn

Bright rich fawn free of black/blue guard hairs shading to white undercolour. Chest to match flanks. Eye circles, inside of ears, underside of jowl, belly and undertail to be white. Faults: Black/blue guard hairs and/or blue undercolour to be considered a serious fault.

Notes – Fawn seems to have become very popular in lops,

unfortunately very few are of a satisfactory colour as the standard clearly states that the fawn should be 'free from black/blue guard hairs' so why do judges keep awarding CC's to rabbits that are clearly full of black/blue guard hairs? This 'act of kindness' (if that is what it is) by judges is only perpetuating the downward spiral of the colour.

Before breeding fawns one should spend considerable time studying the Fawn Rex classes at shows. When the fawn becomes a very light drab colour it can be improved by breeding to orange, however black ticking is a bigger problem and can only be eradicated with patience, perseverance and a strict policy of selective breeding.

21. Gold (A.C.D.ee + rr) (long haired equivalent of orange) go

Cream undercolour, deepening evenly to red-gold top colour, lightly ticked with cream and milk chocolate. Shading milk chocolate. Eyes reddish brown.

Notes – Whow! That would be some lop, could you imagine a Golden German Lop?

22. Golden Glavcot(A.bb C.D.E^s)(brown steel)   gg

A broad band of slate, merging into brown, tipped with light roan, the whole body interspersed with dark brown. Nape of neck light brown, flanks and chest ticking off to a uniform shade slightly lighter than the body, under parts of body cream with slate undercolour. Tail to match body colour on top and belly colour underneath, to be carried in a straight line.

Notes – Not known in lops.

23. Grey (A.B.C.D.E. +u)   gr
24. Iron Grey (aa B. c^{chd}.D.ee)
(long haired equivalent of sallander)   igr

Light grey top colour to carry well down hair shaft to white undercolour. Shading as sooty fawn. Eyes hazel. Faults: Too dark top colour, light tails. White toe nails a serious fault.

Notes – Dilute sooty, common in Cashmere lops and occasionally seen in Dwarf Lops, often confused with seal point. The ruby eye of the seal point is the give-away although there should be quite a distinct difference from the dark sepia brown of the seal point and the sooty shadings of the iron grey.

25. Hare(red agouti) (A.B.C.D.E. +rrr)   bhra

Rich, deep chestnut red, well extended down the sides. Black ticking of a wavy or blotchy appearance, plentiful on body; chest and face free. Feet colour to be solid, free from ticking, pale bars and blotches. Ears, colour to match body and to be carried well inside at the edges, deeply laced with black at the tips.

Notes – See 19.

26. Havana (aa bb C. D. E. +u)   Hv

A rich, dark chocolate with purplish sheen, the colour to go well down the hairs with a pearl-grey undercolour.

Notes – the Havana is the rabbit that chocolate lops have been derived from as they are genetically the same with the Havana's u(unbrous modifier) removed. This has the effect of lightening the colour somewhat. But anyone breeding chocolate lops would do well spending time studying the beautiful Havana. In Germany the Havana coloured Meissner Lop is recognised.

27. Ivory (cc)(satin equivalent of white)   iv

White with satin sheen – the more sheen possible to be considered a beauty and must not be penalised by the judge, eye colour red or blue.

Notes – This is the white version of the fur rabbit the Satin, surely it is only time before someone 'satinises' the lops and puts that lustrous sheen on them.

28. Lilac (aa b C.dd E.)   li

A pinky dove-grey throughout from tip of fur to skin. Blueish tinge a fault.

Notes – The cinderella of the self coloureds and yet there are probably more Lynx around which are Lilac Agoutis. It is difficult to see why the Lilac has not caught on as they can be bred from blending blue and brown together and then concentrating on lilac to lilac but of course the problem of a very small gene pool means that type may be difficult to maintain

29. Lynx (A.bb C.dd E.)   lx

Orange, shot silver. Intermediate colour to be bright orange clearly defined on white undercolour. Tips of fur silver. Belly, eye circles, inside of ears and underside of jowl white. Chest to match flanks. Serious faults: bluish tinge on top, blue undercolour.

Notes – the Lynx is a Lilac Agouti. It is required to have a bright orange intermediate band defined on the white undercolour, achieving this definition is generally very difficult because the very delicate dilute colour means that the orange is usually a pale shade and sometimes runs into the undercolour. When this happens the banding is virtually non-existent and the rabbit will probably look more like a poor fawn than a Lynx. Like other minority colours the Lynx suffers in its development from a small gene pool.

30. Nutria (aa bb C.D.E. +r)   nu

Rich golden brown, colour to go well down the fur, pearl-grey undercolour to reach the skin. Rusty tinge a fault.

Notes – Recognised as a colour for Rex but no longer seen.

31. Opal (A.B.C.dd E.)   op

Top colour pale shade of blue with fawn band between this and a slate blue undercolour. Ears laced blue. Eye circles, underside of tail and belly to be white with slate undercolour.

Notes – sometimes known as the blue agouti, the opal is a dilute colour that has a lighter base colour than the slate of the Agouti and a fawn rather than orange band. Probably the most popular of the minority colours as quite easily bred from blue x agouti crossing; however, being a dilute it suffers from the same problem as the Lynx – weakness in the banding, or banding running into undercolour.

32. Orange (A.C.D.ee +rr)   or

Rich orange free from ticking. Belly white. White or cream undercolour. Eyes hazel.

Notes – a good coloured orange is a truly beautiful sight, but unfortunately one that is rarely seen. All too often the oranges suffer from black guard hairs almost certainly put there by crossing orange with agouti. Many breeders use orange lops to enhance the banding in their agoutis and then when a very good type orange is bred in one of these crossed litters the temptation to show it is too great but unfortunately those well meaning judges keep awarding these poor coloured oranges CC's and thus perpetuate the practice. The only way to eradicate these black guard hairs is by orange to orange matings and selective breeding.

Another frequent problem is that the orange colour does not go down the hair shaft far enough or that the white undercolour comes too far up the hair shaft.

33. Pale Grey (A.B.C.D.E.) pg

Top colour biscuit, carrying well down and merging into pale slate at the base. The whole interspersed with black ticking. The general impression should be biscuit ticked with black on ears, cheeks, body and top of tail. Belly colour white with pale slate undercolour. Eye circle white but non-existent or as small as possible. Body colour should be present on hind feet. Underside of tail white. Eyes hazel.

Notes – a Dutch variant of the agouti that does not have the rufous modifier and therefore does not have the orange banding.

34. Perlfee (A.B.C.dd E.)
(modifiers to be investigated) pf

Top Colour - Greyish blue. Three shades permitted i.e. light, medium and dark, medium shade is preferable. Colour extends evenly all over the body. Eye circles, jaw line, chest and insides of legs are much lighter. Small triangle on nape is brownish in colour. Belly white with blue/grey under fur with a light brown band between belly colour and body colour. Tips of guard hairs are light grey and dark grey. This colour must be clearly seen and give the fur a blue grey pearly look. The pearling must be as regular as possible covering all parts of the body, head, ears, chest, tail and outside of legs.

Under Colour – grey/blue almost two-thirds of fur length, followed by an intermediate colour, brownish in tint. This colour is not to be clearly defined or banded, but must shade into other colours.

Notes – a distinctive colour only seen in the breed that carries its name.

35. Red (A.C.D.ee) (+rrr)   rd

Bright golden red or reddish gold with sheen, free from mealiness. Colour carried well down to skin. Shading slightly lighter on flanks and to the belly with a reddish tint. Eye circles to be white and as small as possible. Ears, face and feet to match body colour.

Notes – a truly magnificent colour seen in the New Zealand Red and the Thrianta, of course it has problems as the triple modifier can cause the colour to gain a yellowish tinge especially in the Thrianta. Surely this is a colour that is crying out to be put into the Dwarf Lop and what a spectacular lop it would be.

36a. Sable (Siamese) Dark (B.c^{chl}c^{chl} D.E.) (+u)   sabd
36b. Sable (Siamese) Medium (B.c^{chl}c^{chl} D.E.)   sabm
36c. Sable (Siamese) Light (B.c^{chl}c D.E.   sabl

Medium – To be a rich sepia on ears, face, back, outside of legs and upper side of tail, the saddle colour shading off to a considerably paler colour on flanks and belly, the dark face colour to shade off from eyes to jowl to blend with the chest and flanks. All blending to be gradual, avoiding any blotches or streaks and consisting of a soft and varied diffusion of sepia shadings. The dark colour on back to extend from head to tail. The chest to be the same colour as the flanks and the whole fur to be absolutely free from white hairs. The undercolour to match the surface colour as closely as possible, following the varied shadings throughout.

Light – as medium, but colour to be 'rich sepia'.

Dark – as medium, but colour to be 'very rich dark sepia'.

NB The main difference in the three colours is the width of saddle in tone and intensity of Sepia colour.

Notes – The various Siamese Sable colours are probably the most popular colours in the Netherland Dwarf but they have not really taken off in the lops. There have been a few very good Dwarf and Miniature Lops in sable and even the odd German Lop. Perhaps it is the difficulty of holding a good adult coat that puts so many off, for whilst they look spectacular as youngsters they have a tendency to become permanently patchy as adults.

Perhaps the biggest problem with breeding Siamese Sables is the presence of too many white hairs; this is usually caused by cross breeding Siamese Sables with Marten Sables. Whilst the progeny of such a cross may well not display the white hairs if these progeny are then bred back into a pure Siamese line then all manner of faults can arise such as white pads, white hairs inside the nose, white hairs in the ears and maybe even white hairs throughout the body.

One can only say that true Siamese Sable to Siamese Sable breeding will avoid introducing colour faults; however, one should avoid dark sable to dark sable matings as the colour just gets darker and darker, so dark sables should only ever be mated to lighter sables.

37. Sallander (aa B.c^{chd}.D.ee) (+u)   sl

Colour of Coat – The base colour is pearl. The guard hairs are blackish brown; the black tips of which cover the whole coat with a veil of pale charcoal colour.

Colour of markings – The markings consist of a base coat, shadings and belly colour and includes the whole body. The belly colour and shadings are sooty (charcoal) coloured, this colour extending over the nose, ears, chest, lower half of shoulders, flanks, rump, top of tail, legs and belly. The shading fades towards the upper body and is strongest on the nose, ears and belly. The head from underneath the eyes to the base of the ears is less heavily shaded. The pattern of the shading should not contain any gaps or breaks (which often occur on the chest underneath the shoulders). The tip of the tail and the underside of the feet may be lighter coloured.

Under and mid colour – The undercolour and mid colour is white.

Notes – Although the Sallander colour is not known in any of the lops they are strangely mentioned in the disqualification for the Sallander where it states that 'pendant ears' are a disqualification 'except in lops'. So perhaps someone involved in the writing of the Sallander breed standard thought that one day someone would develop a Sallander coloured lop, who knows.

Even if there is never a Sallander coloured lop, all those working in sooty fawn lops would do well to study the detail in the description of the Sallander shadings and then take a close look at the sooties that are being shown which certainly do not meet this very detailed requirement.

38. Seal (B.c^{chl}c^{chl} D.E.) (+u)   se

Head and body an even rich dark sepia, shading only slightly paler on lower flanks, chest and belly. Top colour to go well down fur, undercolour to match shadings throughout. Eye colour to reflect deep bluish black.

Notes – Only seen in Rex

39. Seal Point (aa B.c^{chl}.D.ee   sep

A rich sepia brown on ears, nose (mask), feet and tail. Body to be cream with sepia shadings which are gradual to avoid blotches or streaks. Eyes to have a distinct ruby glow, brown eyes are a fault.

Notes – A dilute Siamese Sable. The Seal Point standard only applies to the medium colour but just like the Sables they do come in three shades, light, medium and dark. It is unwise to try to improve the colour of a Seal Point by cross breeding with a Siamese Sable as the dominance of the Sable will prevail and any Seal Points that do come from such a mating are highly likely to suffer from blotchy coats. In recent years Cashmere, Dwarf and even more recently Miniature Lops have all been bred in Seal Point and despite the small gene pool of this minority colour some have been shown that exhibit very good type.

40. Silver-Blue (aa B.C.dd E.) (ticked silvering)   silbu

Body colour, dark slate blue, carried down to the skin.

Notes – This is the definition for the Fancy rabbit the Silver, but lop breeders should take note of this and the next three Silver definitions as they are of course the four colours seen in the Meissner Lop and the Meissner Lop breed standard does not define the colour requirements so this is the best definition we have.

41. Silver-Brown (aa B.C.dd E.) (ticked silvering) silbr

Body colour; a deep rich chestnut, the undercolour to have a top band of the same shade, the base to be a deep blue-black to the skin.

Notes – As for 40 (above)

42. Silver-Fawn (A. C.D.ee) (ticked silvering +rr)   silfn

Body colour, a deep bright orange with undercolour of the same shade carried down to as near the skin as possible.

Notes – As for 40 but the Meissner is known as Yellow.

43. Silver-Grey (aa B.C.D.E.) (ticked silvering) silgr

Body, colour a rich black, the undercolour to blue-black and carried down to the skin.

Notes – As for 40 but the Meissner is known as Black.

44. Smoke Pearl (Siamese) (aa B.C.D.E.) sm

Saddle to extend from nape to tail, to be smoke in colour, shading to pearl grey beige on flanks, chest and belly. Head, ears, feet and upper side of tail to match saddle as near as possible. All shadings to be gradual to avoid blotches or streaks. Undercolour to match surface colour as closely as possible following the varied shadings throughout. Eyes to have a distinct ruby glow.

Faults – Brown eyes, white hairs.

Notes - Smokes are an extremely difficult colour to get right, within the lop breeds they are usually only seen in the Miniature, Dwarf and Cashmere Lops. Of course like all the unusual colours they suffer from a small gene pool so that any faults that creep into the colour are quite difficult to eradicate. Unlike the Siamese Sables the Smokes only have one recognised shade. Therefore if the smoke coloured saddle, required in the standard, starts to get very dark or bluey and lose the required pinky dove tinge then it is difficult to know what to breed into it to bring the required colour back. It is always recommended that it should be the dark doe that is used to a light buck to try and bring the colour back in line and if this fails then another option may be to use a light Siamese Sable buck on a dark Smoke doe. Any good coloured Smoke does resulting from this mating should then be put to as good a Smoke buck as can be found.

From this it will be seen that Smokes are certainly not for beginners or anyone who does not have time to spare and a great deal of patience.

45. Smoke Pearl (Marten) (B.c^{chl}c^{chl} dd E.)
(in three shades as for Sable) smp

The saddle to extend from the nape to tail, to be smoke in colour, shading to pearl grey beige on flanks and chest. Head, ears feet and upper side of tail to match saddle as near as possible. Nose flash permitted, but to be as small as possible. Chest, flanks, rump and feet to be well ticked with longer white hairs, the light nape of the neck to be confined to the triangle behind the ears and to be as small as possible. Eye circles , inside the ears, line of jaws, inside of nostrils, inside of legs and feet, belly and underside of tail and triangle to be white.

Notes – Although the Marten Smoke Pearl is a recognised Fur breed of rabbit the colouring is a marten patterned Smoke and although popular in the Netherland Dwarfs, rarely seen in lops. The Marten pattern is dealt with in the section of this chapter on Patterns.

46. Sooty Fawn (aa B.C.D.ee) sfn

Even shade of orange/fawn top colour to carry well down hair shaft to a bluish/white undercolour. Ears, belly, undertail/tail to be bluish black (sooty), cheeks and flanks to be shaded/topped with sooty tips. Eyes hazel.

Faults – Too dark top colour, light tails. White tails a serious fault.

Notes – Put ten Sooties together and you will probably have ten different coloured lops unless of course they all come from one of the very few breeders who specialise in Sooties and have bred pure sooty to sooty for many generations. It is only pure sooty breeding that can breed Sooties of the right colour, all too often many of those being exhibited fail on the Faults in the standard – dark tops, light or even worse white tails. Many judges seem to ignore the colour faults if the lop is of good type but this is actually not doing the colour any good as it encourages exhibitors to breed and show poorly coloured Sooties.

47. Squirrel (A.B.c^{chd}.dd E.) sq

Undercolour to be dark slate blue at base, intermediate portion pearl with blue narrow line edging. Pearling to be clearly defined. Top grey brightly ticked with blue hairs. Neck fur lighter in colour than body but strictly confined to nape. Flanks and chest ticked with uniform shade of pearl slightly lighter than body. Eye circles light pearl grey. Ears laced with blue.

Notes – the Squirrel is a dilute Chinchilla, and is in effect a blue Chinchilla. The biggest problem with Squirrels is getting the correct banding but as they are compatible with the Chinchilla, and in fact often turn up in pure Chinchilla breeding, they can be bred back into chinchilla lines to improve the definition of the banding.

48. Steel (A.B.C.D.E^s)
(known as Steel Grey in the Dutch)   st

Dark steel grey merging to a slate blue undercoat. The whole interspersed with black guard hairs. Extreme tips of the fur to be tipped with steel blue or grey, the mixture carrying well down the sides, flanks and hind feet. Belly colour will be a lighter shade varying with top colour, underside to tone with belly colour. Ears to match body. Eyes deep hazel.

Faults - (only defined in French Lop). Brown grey or agouti colours in mix a major fault, white belly a disqualification.

Notes- For some inexplicable reason the steel colour is quite popular in the lops. It is not without its problems most of which stem from either white tails and white bellies or a brown tinge to the coat. Most of these problems arise from the mixing of agouti into steel. To the laymen the steel may look very similar to the agouti but in fact the variation of the e gene makes a great deal of difference. Should agouti be put into steels then it is likely that some part of the agouti banding will appear in the steels which is a very undesirable feature. The steel is a beautiful colour when it is correct but it is so easy to get major faults in it and they can be extremely difficult to get rid of.

49. Sussex Cream (aa bb C.dd ee) (ww) (+rr)   sxcr

Pale cream. Undercolour deepening to rich pinkish beige top colour, lightly ticked with lilac and pale cream

Notes – see 50 (below)

50. Sussex Gold (aa bb C.D.ee) (ww) (+rr)   sxgo

Cream undercolour, deepening evenly to red-gold top colour, lightly ticked with cream and milk chocolate. Shading milk chocolate.

Eyes reddish brown.

Notes – It has been suggested in the past that some Miniature Lops have been bred in Sussex Gold, however, when one looks carefully at the weight of the Sussex (7½ – 8½lbs) it would appear extremely unlikely. Certainly the self coloured Lilac would be very similar in appearance to the Sussex Cream, however the Lilac is a self and the Sussex is a shaded colour so they really should not be confused. It could be that a very bright reddish sooty fawn could similarly be confused with the Sussex Gold but of course it could never quite gain enough redness as it would not have the rufous modifier.

51. Thrianta (A. C.D.ee) (+rrr)   thr

Top colour intense reddish golden, very bright, covering the whole of the body including belly, ears, chest, legs and tail. Belly can be paler in colour. Undercolour is paler than top colour, being yellowish.

Slight Faults – Top colour too light. Moulting or mealy coat. Lighter colours or darker colours on chest, flanks and legs.

Serious Faults – Lacking intense colour. Black hairs. Black lacing on ears, different   coloured eyes, white nails, all white belly and undercolour too pale.

Notes – The colour of the Thrianta is genetically identical to the New Zealand Red but the Thrianta is so much nearer to a Dwarf Lop in type (with the obvious differences in the head shape and erect ears) that it can surely only be a matter of time before a dedicated breeder tries to put this wonderful rich colour into a Dwarf Lop and what a stunning Dwarf Lop it would be.

52. Thuringer (aa B.C.D.ee)   thu

The general colour is a yellow ochre or buff (chamois leather) colour. The guard hairs are bluish black colour, which produce a haze of pale charcoal colour.

Notes – The Thuringer is basically the Fur rabbit version of our much loved Sooty Fawns as the colour is genetically the same.

53. Tortoiseshell (aa B.C.D.ee) trt

Formerly known as tortoiseshell, now usually known as 'Sooty

Fawn' or occasionally as 'Madagascar'.

54. Wheaten (A.bb C.dd ee)   wh

Top colour – Wheaten (the fawn or pale yellow colour of wheat), carrying sheen. Shaded lighter on flanks, rump and chest.

Undercolour – Wheaten carried as far to base as possible. Eye circles, inside of ears, undertail, under feet, inside of legs, belly and underside of jowl to be white. Nails to be light horn colour. Eyes to be dark hazel with ruby glow.

Notes – This is surely one colour that has little to offer the lops as we have our beautiful fawns and bright oranges that easily surpass the Wheaten.

55. White – Red Eyed (cc)   rew

As pure white as possible. Eyes ruby red.

Notes – Sounds very easy and probably is the easiest colour to get right, and it is probably because the colour is so easy that there have been many exceptional type rabbits in REW. Anyone who was lucky enough to be at the only ever 6 star show that was held to celebrate the millennium at Stafford may well remember the Fancy Challenge (this was before the days of Lop Challenges), where nearly every rabbit in the challenge was a REW. In fact if the breed came in REW then it was almost certain that it was represented in that fantastic challenge by a REW.

56. White – Blue Eyed (vv)   bew

As pure white as possible. Blue eyes.

Notes – Nowhere near as popular as the REW and generally not of such good type, but there are some fanciers dedicated to these very different white lops.

57. Yellow (A.C.D.ee)   y

An even shade of yellow on ears, cheeks, back and upper part of tail, to be carried well down sides, flanks and feet. Ideally free from chinchillation with no eye circles. Belly colour can be a lighter shade, toning with top colour. Undertail to tone with belly. Eyes hazel.

Notes – This definition is taken from the standard for the Yellow

Dutch but we should take an interest in it as of course yellow is a recognised (although very seldom seen) colour for the Meissner Lop.

Part 2 Breed Patterns

1. Bi-colour (aa C.E.) (+En en)   bic
White body with pattern of one colour only

Notes – Because of rules introduced recently by the Lop clubs regarding the broken pattern it would not be possible to show a bi-colour unless it conformed to the butterfly pattern (see notes on butterfly pattern below).

2. Blanc de Hotot (aa C. E.) (+du du +En En)   bdh
No pigmentation whatever on body except for eye circles. Fur snow white, dense – soft and lustrous. Guard hairs numerous and obvious giving a frosty appearance. Nails non-pigmented pinkish white.

Faults – Guard hairs not sufficiently obvious. Eye circles a little irregular or a little too wide 3-5mm.

Disqualifications – No guard hairs. Incomplete eye circles or too wide. Lashes and lids not black. Wall eyes. Colour marks on white fur. Black nails.

Notes – Not seen in lops at present but not beyond the ingenuity of the enterprising breeder looking for a challenge.

3. Butterfly (+En en)   bfly
Pattern to be white and any other allowed colour. The white markings around the nose to be such that leaves a distinct butterfly smut or as a shading on the sooty-fawn. Ears to be coloured. The white should extend upwards from the chin and chest over the shoulders with two spots one each side on the shoulders called shoulder spots. A small 'V' on the shoulders is permissible. No white to be present in the general body colouring. The belly to be white but teat spots permissible. White on nose or smut is a pattern fault.

Faults – Too many white hairs on nose or top lip.

Disqualification – Putty nose.

Notes – In 2001 the B.R.C. accepted the Broken Pattern for the Mini Rex, which was immediately seen as a disaster by the Lop fraternity who had spent many years perfecting the Butterfly Pattern. The root of the problem was that the Lop Breed Standards had allowed for 'any accepted colour or pattern' therefore this decision to allow the broken pattern meant that any broken would now be acceptable and all those years of dedicated breeding to perfect the butterfly pattern were in an instant made irrelevant. The Lop Clubs were quick to react and at their next Annual General Meetings all voted an amendment into their rules banning the broken pattern. The years of dedicated work by the butterfly specialists was preserved.

The standard for the Butterfly pattern is very specific and any lop that does not meet the stringent requirements of the standard is unacceptable. Specialising in butterflies is not for the faint hearted; it takes many, many generations of breeding well marked specimens to fix the pattern and breed true. Breeding from poorly marked butterflies will almost certainly result in the majority of the progeny being poorly marked.

4. Californian (aa $c^{ch} c^{ch}$ E.)

Coloured nose, ears, feet and tail. Colour as dark as possible. Coloured spots on dewlap to be small and confined to dewlap only. Body colour to be pure white.

Faults – Eyes faded in colour. Light toe nails or nails. Coloured spots on dewlap out of proportion, light shading in the coloured section due to moult.

Disqualification – One or more white toenails. Colour extending on to the body of the pelt above junction of the front legs with the body, white spots in coloured fur. Absence of colour on nose, ears, feet or tail.

Notes – Recognised in three colours:

Chocolate – markings are milk chocolate coloured.

Blue – markings a clear shade of slate blue extending to the skin, even coloured points.

Lilac – markings to be an even pink shade of dove extending to the skin, even coloured points.

The Californian rabbit is a large version of the Himalayan; although the Netherland Dwarf breeders have bred the pattern it is unknown in the Lops.

5. Dalmatian (+En en)   dal

Coat is not pigmented, that is to say white all over. The pattern consists of numerous little coloured patches covering the body, head and ears. To be bi-coloured – white body with pattern of one colour only or tri-coloured – white body with pattern of two colours (i.e. black patches and fawn patches).The patches can only be, black, blue, brown, orange or fawn. The colour to be carried down as far as possible. Eyes and ears to match appropriate colours; solid ears, eye circles and smut are allowable.

Faults – Not enough coloured patches.

Disqualification – Pattern too much like that of a butterfly or an English i.e. with the resemblance of a saddle.

Notes – Tri-coloured Dalmatian Dwarf Lops were certainly exhibited at the London Championship Show at the turn of the century but are now rarely seen. With development of any new pattern it takes a long time and many generations to put the pattern in and then get the type back and it is often this long struggle that sees even the most determined breeder fall by the wayside. Let's hope we will see this beautiful pattern on lops back on the show bench before too long.

6. Dutch (+du du)   du

a. **Blaze** – Wedge shaped, carrying up to a point between the ears.

b. **Cheeks** – As round as possible and as near the whiskers without touching. Also covering the line of the jawbone.

c. **Clean Neck** – Means free from coloured fur immediately behind the ears.

d. **Saddle** – Is the junction between white and coloured fur on the back. This line to continue right round the animal in an even straight line.

e. **Undercut** – Continuation of the saddle. To be as near up to the front legs as possible without touching them.

f. **Stops** – White markings on the hind feet about 3.17cm (1¼ ins) in length and to cut cleanly round the foot in a similar manner to the saddle and undercut.

Disqualification – Wrong coloured eyes. Discoloured or wall eyes (pale blue iris), specked eyes (pale blue spots or specks in the iris). Coloured fur on the white part or white patches on the coloured parts. Flesh markings (usually on the ears).

Notes - There have certainly been Dutch pattern Netherland Dwarfs for a number of years but as yet no one has taken on the challenge of putting the pattern into a lop. There really is no reason why it cannot be done and it will just take someone with the time and dedication, and probably a bit of a death wish, when you see just how difficult it is for even the Dutch specialists to get it right.

7. English (+En en)   en
Head Markings –

a. Perfect Butterfly Smut

b. Circle around eyes

c. Cheek spots to be clear from eye circles (either cheek spot missing deemed to be a serious fault)

d. Ears neat and clear from white

Body markings –

a. Unbroken saddle, to be herring-boned and clear in any distinct colour, from base of ears to tip of tail

b. Body and loin markings to be nicely broken up and not to catch the saddle

c. Chain markings, to be as even as possible on each side

d. Leg markings, one distinct spot on each leg

e. Belly or teat spots (there should be six)

Disqualification – Both cheek spots touching eye circles. Putty noses.

Notes – A dedicated band of Netherland Dwarf breeders have for many years been trying to put the English pattern into their breed, they call them E.M.Ds. (English marked Netherland Dwarfs). The English pattern is generally regarded in the Rabbit Fancy as the most difficult, and probably the most impossible, of all patterns to perfect. Whilst there can be no doubt that the E.M.L. (English marked

Lop) would be a challenge perhaps it is a challenge too far for the foreseeable future as there are still so many other colours and patterns that need to be worked on in the lops.

8. Fox (a^{t}a^t c^{chd}. E.)

Body colour to be black, blue, chocolate or lilac and to go down the fur as far as possible with undercolour of appropriate selfcolour. Chest, flanks and feet to be well and evenly ticked with silver-tipped guard hairs. Any extension of the ticking up the side and/or over the back to be considered a beauty and not a fault. Eye circles as neat as possible, a pea spot in front of the base of each ear. Inside of ears, line of jaw, underside of tail and belly, all to be white. Triangle behind ears to be white but as small as possible.

Notes – Although there are many fine fox patterned lops around the otter lops would seem to be more popular; there can be no obvious reason for this as a good type Black Fox is certainly a most stunning animal. Like the otters the self coloured foxes can be inter-bred with each other but should only be bred to with any other colour in order to improve the all important silver-tipped ticking. The nape of the neck and the ticking on a young Fox patterned lop may well exhibit a tawny tinge causing the inexperienced breeder to believe they have bred otters from fox matings, however the tinge will disappear when the lop matures and acquires its adult coat.

9. Harlequin (aa C.e^{j}e^j)   hq

Head – To be equally divided, one side black the other side golden orange.

Ears – One ear to be black the other to be golden orange. The black ear on the golden orange side of the face, and vice-versa.

Legs – One front leg golden orange, the other black. One hind leg black, the other golden orange the reverse side to the front.

Body – To be banded in black and orange as clearly defined as possible. It should not be considered a fault if the bands are broken at the vental or dorsal lines. Belly colour may be lightish.

Colour – All four self colours, black, blue, brown (chocolate) and lilac are recognised. The black parts to be as dense a black as possible with the coloured parts being as dense and bright as possible.

Notes – A few years ago harlequin patterned Dwarf and Miniature Lops were regularly seen at shows, but their popularity seems to have dwindled in recent years. They will always be a minority pattern due to the low percentage of kits born displaying the required mix of black and the other colour but they are interesting if somewhat of a novelty pattern and it would be a shame to see them disappear from our show benches.

10. Himalayan (aa c^{ch}c^{ch}E.)   hi
a. **Ears** – Black
b. **Nose** – Black, even and well up between eyes.
c. **Front Feet** – Black, markings well up.
d. **Hind Feet** – Black, to correspond markings well up hocks.
e. **Eyes** – Bright pink.
f. **Remainder of colour** – pure white.
Disqualification – White toenails.

Notes - All four self colours, black, blue, chocolate and lilac are recognised. A pattern seen in Poles and Netherland Dwarfs but not yet put into Lops.

11. Magpie (aa c^{chd} e^j e^j)   mag
As for Harlequin (No.9) but the black is replaced with white.

Notes – All four self colours, black, blue, brown (chocolate) and lilac are recognised. As with the Harlequin, Magpie lops are occasionally seen on the show bench but not often enough.

12. Marten (a^{t}a^t c^{chl}c^{chl} E.)
The chest, flank, rump and feet to be well ticked with longer white hairs, any extension of white ticking over sides and rump to be considered an added beauty and not a fault, but ears and saddle to be free of white hairs. The light nape of neck to be confined to triangle behind ears and to be as small as possible; colour to match flanks. Eye circles, inside of ears, line of jaw, belly and underside of tail to be white. General undercolour to match surface colour as closely as possible, following the general shadings throughout.

Notes – The Marten pattern is seen in sable and smoke coloured rabbits. Considering that both sable and smokes are minority colours in the Lops it will not be surprising that there are few Martens around; this is in complete contrast to the Netherland Dwarfs where the Marten pattern is perhaps the most popular of all patterns.

13. Otter (a^{t}a^t C. E.) (+rr)

Colour black, blue, chocolate or lilac uniform colour to cover back and sides. The underbody or belly to be creamy white and also underside of tail. A tan border to divide the colour and white and encircle nostrils and under chin. A mixture of body colour and tan covers feet. Tan ticking to the chest, flanks and rump, extended ticking to be an added beauty not a fault. Tan eye circle and nape of neck. The ears to be body colour bordered on outside with tan which covers inside of ears.

Fault – A distinct lack of tan from proper parts.

Notes – The otter pattern is extremely popular especially in the Miniature Lops where there have been some exceptional rabbits exhibited over the years. The blacks and blues are by far the best type and most popular; perhaps it is because there are fewer Chocolates and Lilacs that there just is not the gene pool required to improve the type.

Otters were originally bred from Agouti cross Marten Sables and can now suffer from the dominant Otter gene that causes white hairs to appear up the nose, on the face and body parts. It can also cause a tan brindling, particularly on the face, to occur. These faults can be eradicated by breeding an otter doe to a self coloured buck (black otter to black buck etc.), however any self coloured offspring that result from this mating should go straight to the pet shop as they will introduce more colour faults into the already difficult self. Unfortunately too many exhibitors ignore this advice and we see Otters that fail colour and selfs, particularly blacks, with a tan tinge being exhibited all the time. It would appear that the only way that this can be stopped is for judges to start withholding CC's and make sure that only those lops without colour faults are kept within the Fancy and bred from.

14. Papillon (+En en)   pap
Pattern of the Head –

a. the butterfly or pattern of the nose; this is well defined, the two wings full, on each side touching only lightly the edges of the lower jaw. The fork in the centre of the nose is lightly rounded.

b. the eye circles; each eye is circled by a coloured eye circle, quite regular, which does not touch the other parts of the pattern on either side.

c. the cheek spots; are rounded, and situated below the eye circles, without touching them.

d. the pattern of the ears; the ears are completely coloured and clean cut at the base.

Pattern of the Body –

a. the saddle stripe; it commences at the back of the ears and extends over the whole back to the tail.

b. pattern on the rump; a group of at least three spots on each side, towards the rear of the flanks and on the thighs, not touching the saddle. The ideal is 6 to 8 spots on each side. Markings on the belly and legs are ignored.

Colour – The base colour is white. All recognised colours are admissible. Eye colour to match that of each recognised colour. The claws are not coloured.

Faults – small spots on the head, the butterfly insufficiently defined, the edges of the lips uncoloured or flesh coloured; a small break in the saddle stripe from in front of the shoulder blades to the base of the tail; pattern on flanks too weak, too strong or irregular; one isolated chain spot; the spots on the flanks joined up.

Disqualifications – putty nose, the lips white, the saddle stripe visibly broken between the shoulder blades and base of the tail, absence of one or both cheek spots, the pattern on the head joined up, white patches in the coloured fur, the lower jaw completely covered by the wings of the butterfly, eye circles not closed, less than three spots on any one flank, two or more isolated chain spots, incorrect eye colour.

Notes - Not seen in Lops at present.

15. Rhinelander (aa C. e^{j}e^j) (+En en)   rh

Pattern of the Head – the butterfly with well-rounded body – wings regularly spread extending under the lower jaw. Circle around eye regular and closed. Patches on cheeks round or oval – separated from eye circles. Ears entirely coloured. At the base the colours separate on the white and are as neat as possible.

The pattern of the Body – the saddle unbroken from nape to point of tail. The patches on the flanks regular – 6 to 8 spots each side. Not too big and separated from each other. Spots on belly and legs are ignored. The two colours are a must for the saddle. Black and yellow patches are a must for the flanks. Nails pinkish white.

Colour – White with markings of black and yellow making up the pattern.

Each of the patches may be mono or bi-coloured, with the exception of the cheek patches which are of one colour.

Faults – outline of butterfly wings uneven, body of butterfly not distinct. Marks other than cheek spots. Wall eyes. White at ear bases. Break in saddle. Saddle touching flank patches. One spot on each side or two spots on one side only. Patches on flanks too wide or too small. White hairs in coloured patches. Different colours in one spot.

Disqualifications – deformed butterfly pattern, butterfly touching eye circles, extending out to the ears. Incomplete eye circles. White tips on ears. Flank pattern encroaching on the saddle. Less than three patches on one flank. More than two spots on each side. Patches of one colour only with the exception of the cheek spots. Sooty fawn colour. White hairs in the butterfly. Eyes of different colour.

Notes – Not seen in Lops at present.

16.   Siamese (aa $c^{chl}c^{chl}$ E.)   si

Saddle to extend from nape to tail, shading to flanks, chest and belly. Head, ears, feet and upper side of tail to match saddle as near as possible. All shadings to be gradual to avoid blotches and streaks. Underclour to match surface colour as closely as possible following the various shadings throughout. Eyes to have a distinct ruby glow, brown eyes are a fault.

Notes – the Siamese pattern is a shaded pattern found on sables and smokes. The Siamese sables come in three shades: light, medium and dark. Perhaps the biggest problem with Siamese sables is the presence of white hairs that have been introduced through the crossing with Martens. The crossing of Siamese sables and Martens can be done but a simple rule must be followed to retain the shading and colour requirements; the Siamese progeny of the Siamese/Marten cross should never be put back into a pure Siamese blood line. This is because the Siamese progeny from the cross will carry 50% Marten genes and whilst the first generation progeny from the crossed Siamese to true Siamese may breed true subsequent litters will mix the genes so that the white hair problem will become difficult to eradicate from the line. The same rule applies to Siamese smokes and Marten smokes.

17. Tan (a^{t}a^t C. E.) (+rrr)   tn

Colour – No other colour but black and tan. No white or foreign colour amongst either black or tan. The colour both in the black and tan should reach right down to the skin.

Distribution of Black (body colour) and Tan (markings) – The head and cheeks to be black, that same colour reaching right up to nose point, but with a ring of tan round each eye (eye circles). The shoulders (except immediately behind the ears) saddle, back rump, sides and upper part of tail black. All should be free from brindling, except sides and sides of rump, which should be thickly laced with long tan hairs (side ticking). The nostrils, jowl, chest, belly, flanks and under part of tail should be one solid mass of deep golden tan, inclining to red or mahogany tint, brightness of tan to be of greater importance than actual tint. The tan should be quite clear from any mixture of soot or body colour. The shoulders or neck immediately behind the ears should be tan, wide near the ears and tapering to a fine point towards back, thus forming a triangle. This should be large enough to be partly seen even if the rabbit's head is up. From the base of the triangle near the ears the tan should descend and if possible to meet the tan on the tan chest, thus forming a kind of band or collar around the neck. At the root of the ears, viewed from the front, two tan spots, known as 'pea spots' should be seen, the larger these are the better.

Ears – Outside jet-black, inside laced with tan all round (if the whole of the insides are tan, so much the better). Ears free from white tips, white hairs or brindling.

Hind legs – The outer part of leg reaching from foot to rump - black, inner part - rich tan. The division between black and tan should form an unbroken line right up the leg, free from raggedness. The tan on the inner side to be quite free from spots, pencilling, bars or black. Toes wholly tan.

Front legs – The lower front part, black as free from brindle as possible. The hinder part and toes wholly tan.

Penalties (faults) – brindle white or grey hairs amongst body colour (except on sides of body, where long tan hairs should be plentiful). White ear edges, white or brindled hairs on outside of ears. Smudgy nose point. Brindled front legs. Black or blue bars, pencilling or spots on tan or hind legs and indistinct line of division along same.

Disqualification – Putty nose, white tufts in armpits.

Notes – Colour variants black, blue, chocolate and lilac are all accepted.

The black tan is probably the most spectacular of all rabbits when in full coat and surely it cannot be too long before someone takes up the challenge and gives us a tan lop. What a winner that would be.

18. Tri-colour (Dutch) (aa C. $e^j e^j$)   tri

One cheek must be orange, other cheek black with ears black on orange side and orange on black cheek side. Blaze is white. It commences at a point starting near the ear roots and gradually widens evenly passing between the eyes on to the neck and nape. This white must be as wide as possible. Must not pass between the ears. The saddle must make a true ring around the body. The coloured half must be banded as regularly as possible with alternating bands of black and orange. Stops regular.

Colours – also recognisable, blue to replace black, chocolate to replace black.

Disqualification – Discoloured or wall eyes (pale blue iris), specked eyes (pale blue spots or specks on the iris). Coloured fur on the white part or white patches on the coloured parts. Flesh markings (usually on the ears).

Notes – This pattern is not seen in Lops.

Chapter 16
The Future of the Lop

Above: Lionhead Lop exhibited at Bradford Ch Show. Fur & Feather photo library

Below Velveteen Lop F2 generation. Bred and photographed by the author

One hundred and fifty years ago there was one breed of lop. One hundred years ago in Britain there was still one breed of lop, fifty years ago there were three breeds of lop and now there are eight breeds.

How many will there be in fifty, one hundred or one hundred

and fifty years from now? Of course none of us know the answer to that.

Lops have certainly become extremely popular as pets and the pet rabbit population is expanding rapidly, however they have also become increasingly popular on the show bench while numbers of exhibitors and exhibits of other breeds have decreased quite dramatically. There are those pessimists around who believe there will not be an exhibition Fancy in fifty years time; who knows, they could be right – but surely the lop has got such a hold that it is here to stay.

Giant Cashmere Lop, bred by Rob and Maggie Ricketts

The big difference the loss of the Fancy would make to the lop is that the development of new breeds, colours and patterns would cease, as would the perfecting of existing breeds. In fact quite the reverse would happen as standards and excellence would quickly disappear as cross breeding was allowed to become the norm.

If the lop is to go on to greater heights the Fancy must not only survive but completely turn around from its present position. Only when there is a strong vibrant Fancy that is continually attracting new members with new demands and new ideas and enthusiasm will the lop go forward. Only a very small percentage of Fanciers will ever have the inclination, dedication and determination to perfect new colours and develop new breeds and the smaller the Fancy gets the less people there are attracted to the task.

There are undoubtedly a great many challenges for those who have the resources and desire. One only has to look at a beautiful young Black Tan – as its breeder goes forward to collect another Best in Show award – surely a Tan Lop would sweep the boards (providing of course the type had been perfected as well as the colour).

There are so many beautiful colours and patterns that have not yet been put into our lops, but without a vibrant Fancy will the people ever be found who want to carry out the work?

There are currently three new breeds of lop in some stage or other of development in Britain. Certainly the most advanced of these is the Lionhead Lop; it has been worked on now for a number of years and is very close to gaining B.R.C. recognition. The other two new lops are still a long way away from being recognised.

The Giant Cashmere Lop, a cashmere version of the French Lop, has a few followers but has just as many against the development of such a breed on the grounds that there could not be pet homes for any rabbits that do not come up to the exacting show standards. Whether the Giant Cashmere Lop is ever developed to gain recognition is anyone's guess.

The third lop under development and in its very early stages in this country is the Velveteen Lop; a smaller, rex coated version of the English Lop. Much work has been carried out in America on the Velveteen Lop over the last ten years and it is very near to gaining recognition there but very little has been done on this side of the Atlantic. Again it will take a group of dedicated Fanciers to develop this new breed.

The future of lops in Britain is inextricably linked to the future of the British Fancy. If the Fancy continues to decline, for what ever reason, then almost certainly the development of the Lop breeds, colours and patterns will cease to progress or, even worse, go backwards.

Perhaps we have already seen the halcyon days of the lop. Let us hope not and that the Fancy will recover from its present malady allowing the lop exhibitors to thrive and take these wonderful rabbits forward to greater heights.

Glossary of Common Terms

The definitions given below have been stated as applied to Lops in particular and some may have slightly different connotations when applied to rabbits other than Lops.

Adult – a lop of 5 months or over is considered an adult for show purposes (note: this does not mean that the lop is ready for breeding).

Adult Coat – The rabbit's mature coat that is produced for the first time when the rabbit is between 6 – 9 months old.

AC – Any colour

Ad – Adult

Albino – A red eyed white lop that is recessive to colour that will always breed true when mated together, but may genetically contain the gene for any colour or marking which is masked by the double dominant white gene. Thus when crossed with a coloured rabbit the outcome can be difficult to predict.

All Rounder Judge – A Senior Judge who is equally qualified in all breeds.

Any Colour – Any colour or pattern that conforms to the colour or pattern of recognised breeds.

AOC – Any other colour, a term used when there is not a specific class for a particular colour.

AOV – Any other variety, a term used when there is not a specific class for a particular breed.

Area Club – A club, the activities of which are confined to one geographical area.

ASS – Adult Stock Show.

Astringent – A property of some plants useful in scours in that it opposes any laxative effect.

AV – Any Variety, a term usually used in the Challenges – AV Lop.

Baby Coat – The early coat, usually up to 3-5 months of age.

Bagginess – Looseness of pelt, particularly around the rump on older lops.

Banding – A hair shaft having various colours, particularly in the agouti pattern lops.

Barred Feet – Lighter stripes on coloured feet, a common fault on agouti patterned, chinchilla and fox patterned lops.

Barrel-length – Long and round in the body.

Barrenness – The inability of a doe to bear young, infertility.

Base Colour – Colour of the hair shaft closest to the body.

BEW – Blue Eyed White.

BIS (BiS) – Best in Show

Bloat – A condition where the stomach and intestines of the lop fill with gas, a potentially fatal condition that is extremely difficult to cure.

Bloom – The vitality and finish of a coat in good condition. The kind of coat we all seek to achieve in exhibition lops.

Bold Eye – A prominent, full eye – a sign of a healthy lop.

Bowed Legs – Usually seen when the front legs are bent like a bow – curved outward in the middle, may rarely be seen in the hind legs. A particular fault in some English Lops.

Breeder – The owner of the dam of a lop at the time of its birth. Can be an important definition when entering Breeder Classes.

Breeders' Class – A class confined to exhibits bred by the exhibitor (see Breeder above).

Brindling – Coloured or white hairs interspersed in the desired colour. Brindling is a common fault in sooty fawns and across the noses of otters.

BRC – British Rabbit Council.

Broken Coat – Where the coat is affected by moult, exposing the undercoat or new coat coming through.

Broody Doe – A doe ready for mating.

Buck – A male rabbit.

Butterfly Nose Marking – The coloured butterfly-like pattern on the nose of a butterfly. There should be no white in the upper lip and no colour in the lower lip.

Butterfly – A very specific pattern that must carry the butterfly nose markings (see Chap 16).

Carriage – The way and style in which a lop bears itself.

Castration – Removal of the male organs of reproduction.

Challenge Certificate (CC) – Certificate awarded at BRC Star Shows to rabbits of outstanding merit and registered with the BRC in the name of the exhibitor. These certificates must be retained for

Championship claims and will not be replaced if lost.

Charlie – A term applied to a rabbit that is extremely light in colour, usually a butterfly that has insufficient body markings but usually retains its coloured ears and a 'Charlie Chaplin moustache' instead of the full butterfly face marking. Not a showable colour.

Cheeks – Rounded area between eyes and jaw.

Chest - The front of the rabbit between the forelegs and the chin.

Chinchillation – A banded undercolour.

Chopped – Applied to type. Having the rump cut off abruptly and falling vertically to the tail instead of being rounded.

Clean Cut – The line of demarcation between markings being clear, with no tendency of one to run into another.

Club Judge – Judges elected to Specialist Clubs as qualified to judge specific breeds, whose awards will be recognised for Club Championships and Special Prizes.

Cobby – A short and stocky body type which is close coupled and very compact.

Condition – The physical state of the rabbit with reference to its health.

Cowhocks – Hocks that bend inwards causing the foot to turn outwards.

Cross-breeding – The breeding together of two different breeds or colours of rabbit.

Definition – In Chinchillas and Agouti pattened, the clear line of demarcation between the pearling and the undercolour.

Dewlap – A pouch of loose skin under the neck – usually found in does and undesirable in show lops.

Diplomas – Offered at BRC approved shows to Section or Best in Show winners. (The Best Lop or Lop Diploma was introduced 2001).

Doe – A female rabbit.

Dewclaw – An extra toe on the inside of the front legs.

Drags – Intrusions of colour into white areas of fur.

Ear Label – A small sticky label bearing the rabbit's pen number. It is stuck either between the shoulder blades or on the inside of the ear.

Ear Lacing – A coloured line of fur that outlines the sides and tips of the ears.

Eye Circle – The contrasting colour circle of fur next to the eye.

Fancier/The Fancy – A member of the (rabbit) Fancy. OED definition – 'The art or practice of breeding animals so as to develop particular points'.

Fancy Section – Section restricted to Fancy rabbits only: Lops used to be part of this section and are still included in it at some small shows or in areas where there are few lops.

Feathering – A division of white and colour in a pattern that is irregular or lacking in clear demarcation.

Fine Boned – A term used to describe bone structure; usually derogatory in lops that should be strong boned and thick set.

Finish – The desired degree of perfection in condition of coat ('a finished rabbit').

Firm Condition – The desired condition where the skeleton is well covered with firm flesh.

First Cross (F1) – The immediate offspring of two pure breeds mated together.

Fly Back - The coat when stroked against the lie 'flies back'; a fault in Lops that require a roll back coat.

Fore Feet – Front Feet.

Foster Mother – A doe used in the rearing of another doe's litter.

Foreign Colour – Any colour of fur, nails or eyes differing from that required by the Standard.

Frosted Nose – The sprinkling of hair found on the nose of some Tan-patterned varieties especially Foxes which give a frosted appearance. It is a fault.

Full Coat – Adult coat free from moult – a highly desirable condition.

Gestation – The period of pregnancy. Usually between 30 – 32 days.

Ghost – A very light chinchilla with wide pearling and little or no undercolour.

Glossy – A bright coat that reflects the light, as opposed to dull and lifeless appearance of the fur.

Groin – The area between the hind legs and the belly.

Guard Hairs – The longer and stronger hairs found in the coat; the presence of guard hairs is particularly important in the roll back coat.

Hock – The last joint on a hind leg.

Inbreeding – The mating together of very close relations such as father and daughter, mother to son, brother to sister.

In Kindle – Pregnant doe.

Intermediate Coat – The coat prior to the full adult coat that generally appears about 4-5½months old.

Iris – The coloured portion of the eye, surrounding the pupil.

Kindling – The birth of a litter.

Lactating - The production of milk by the doe.

Line Breeding – The mating together of rabbits of the same strain, but not so close as that of inbreeding.

Litter – The youngsters born from a single pregnancy.

Lop Ear – Pendulous ears, carried below horizontal rather than upright.

Malocclusion – Teeth having the lower incisors extending in front of the upper incisors or meeting with no overlap. This condition may be hereditary and maloccluded rabbits should not be bred from.

Mandolin – Having the appearance of a mandolin laid face down. Body arch starting at the back of the shoulders rather than the nape of the neck, a particularly important feature of English Lops.

Marked Rabbit – A scab, scar or mark (but specifically not a vaccine mark), usually damage, a deformity or mutilation that identifies a rabbit. A disqualification.

Matted – Wool or fur tangled in thick mass, especially in Cashmeres.

Mealy Colour - A lighter shade of the required colour that gives an almost speckled appearance and is undesirable.

Moult – The casting of one coat and the growth of new fur.

Muzzle – The lower part of the face and nose.

Open Coat – Coat lacking ability to return to its natural position when stroked towards the head.

Outcrossing – Breeding unrelated rabbits or lines within the same breed.

Parasite – Another organism that lives on, or within, the host animal. Examples are mange, mites, lice and fleas.

Pearling – The lighter band of colour in the chinchilla coat which comes next to the undercoat.

Pea Spots – Two spots at the root of the ears in tan pattern varieties when viewed from the front.

Pedigree - The recording of parentage.

Pendant Ears – Essential in lops.

Points – The coloured extremities of the rabbit.

Pseudo Pregnancy – A doe exhibiting all the signs of pregnancy but producing no young.

Putty Nose – White spot on the nose extremity. A disqualification.

Racy – When applied to lops a derogatory term meaning long in body and lacking breadth, especially in the shoulders.

Rat Faced – Narrow skull and head.

REW – Red Eyed White.

Ring – Metal band, sold by the BRC to paid up members only and fitted to one of the rear legs of the rabbit. All rabbits (except tattooed imports) must be fitted with a ring when young so that they can be shown later in their lives.

Roll Back Coat – A gradual return to the normal position of the fur when stroked from rump to shoulders, a requirement of the lops coat.

Roman Nose – A nose whose bridge is so comparatively high as to form a slightly convex line from the forehead to nose tip. Especially pronounced in English Lops and less so in German Lops.

Rump – The hindquarters of the rabbit.

Run – An intrusion of white colour into a coloured marked area on a marked breed.

Rusty Colour – As applied to blacks and blues, a rusty tinge that can be caused by sunlight, cross breeding or at certain stages of the moult. Undesirable.

Saddle – The whole upper portion of the back.

Scours – Diarrhoea.

Screw Tail – Tail twitched to one side, particularly a problem in English Lops with their very long tails.

Self – The rabbit being the same colour all over. Undercolour usually paler. REW, BEW, Black, Blue, Brown (Chocolate) and Lilac.

Shaded Pattern – the pattern found in Siamese Sable, Siamese Smokes, Seal Points and Sooty Fawns.

Shadings – Variation in shades from darker on the saddle to lighter on the sides, especially in sables and smokes.

Shape – The general conformation of a lop's overall appearance, as shown by body structure. Synonym for type.

Sheen – Lustrous effect – brilliance of coat when in peak condition.

Shoulder – That portion of the body from the neck back through the 5th rib and the upper joint of the foreleg.

Silvering – The mixture in the coat of white tipped guard hairs, as desired in the Meissner Lop but even a few are a fault in all other lops.

Slate – The bottom colour in Agouti and Chinchilla, Black, Blue and Brown.

Smellers – The whiskers.

Smut – Darker nose markings.

Snipey – Narrow elongated head.

Sore Hock – An ulceration above the footpad. Caused on the back hocks by thin bedding or stamping.

Speck Eye – Small white specks in the iris of the eye.

Standard – Standards are submitted to the BRC for scrutiny and approval before being accepted for the Official Breed Standards Book. The Standard allocates a total of 100 points for the judge to allocate to the various attributes required for the breed.

Strain – A genetically related bloodline possessing distinguishing characteristics such as type, colour or coat, and the ability to pass the characteristic to the offspring.

Stud – A collection of rabbits where breeding usually takes place.

Stud Buck – A buck used for mating, usually no longer used for showing.

Tan Pattern – The pattern found in Fox and Marten Sable Lops.

Ticking – Hairs of a different colour to the main coat, generally shown by the guard hairs only.

Tortoiseshell (Tort) – An alternative term for Madagascar or Sooty Fawn.

Triangle – A small area behind the ears, in the shape of a triangle, that is generally lighter in colour than the rest of the coat. A feature of Tan and Agouti pattered lops.

Trimming – The illegal removal of hairs, etc to improve the look of the lop.

Type – The appearance and conformation of the lop.

Undercolour – The colour at the base of the fur shaft or next to the skin.

Variety – A distinct breed such as English Lop, German Lop, Cashmere Lop as opposed to the various colours of a breed.

Vent Disease – A venereal disease in rabbits that affects both sexes.

VHD – Viral Haemorrhagic Disease.

Wall Eye – An eye that is whitish on the surface (cornea) of the eye. Having a milky film over the eye.

Weaning – The removal of youngsters from the doe.

White Toenail - A nail without pigmentation, Showing only pink cast in the blood vessel.

Woolliness – A type of fur showing the character of wool rather than fur, a fault in the Cashmere coat.

Wry Neck – Carriage of the head to one side at an angular plane, instead of the normal carriage in a vertical plane, often caused by a deep seated middle ear infection.

Recommended Reading

The following titles may be of interest to the lop fancier; regrettably several – including the classic *The Domestic Rabbit* – are out of print. Source second-hand bookshops or the internet, or contact Veronica Mayhew, Trewena, Behoes Lane, Woodcote, Nr Reading, RG8 OPP (01491 680743) email: *veronica.mayhew@virgin.net* who specialises in old and out of print rabbit books and prints.

Fur & Feather stocks around thirty recommended rabbit titles in their postal bookshop; for a copy of their book list telephone 01473 652 789 or contact the address on facing page.

A Fancier's Guide to the Netherland Dwarf
by *Phil Birch*
Coney Press 1997

All the Lop Club Year Books

Biology & Medicine of Rabbits and Rodents
by *John E Harkness & Joseph W Wagner*
USA 2nd Ed 1983

BRC Breeds Standard 2001 – 2005
BRC 2001

Colour Inheritance in Small Livestock
by *Roy Robinson*
Fur & Feather 1968

Diseases of the Domestic Rabbit by *Lieve Okerman*
Blackwell 1988

Encyclopaedia of Rabbits and Rodents
by *Esther Verhoef Verhallen*
Rebo Productions 1977

Fur and Feather – back issues

Keeping Rabbits
by *CF Snow*
W&G Foyle 1958

Lop Rabbits as Pets
by *Sandy Crooke*
TFH Publications 1986

Rabbit Breeding for Perfection
by *AE Williams*
Acacia Press 1992

Rabbitlopedia
by *Meg Brown & Virginia Richardson*
Ringpress Books Ltd 2000
Rabbits – Health, Husbandry & Diseases
by *Virginia Richardson*
Blackwell Science Ltd 2000

Read About Rabbits No.4 French and Dwarf Lop
by *Peter Ralphes*
Winckley Publishing 1983

The Beginner's Guide to the Cashmere Lop
by *Jean Wolstenholme*
Coney Press 1995

The Domestic Rabbit 5ᵗʰ Edition
by *John Sandford*
Blackwell Science 1996

UK Rabbit Governing Body, Magazine, Clubs

British Rabbit Council, Purefoy House, 7 Kirkgate, Newark, Notts. NG24 1AD. Phone 01636 676042. Fax 01636 611683. Email: info@thebrc.org. Web Site: www.thebrc.org.
   The BRC is the governing body of the rabbit fancy, issuing show support to affiliated clubs and rings to its members. It publishes the Breed Standards book.

Fur & Feather inc. RABBITS, Elder House, Chattisham, Ipswich, Suffolk IP8 3QE.
   Fur & Feather inc RABBITS is the official journal of the British Rabbit Council.
Phone 01473 652 789 or 01473 652 354. Fax 01473 652 788.
Email: furandfeather@btinternet.com.
Web Sites: www.furandfeather.co.uk and www.rabbitsmagazine.co.uk.

Clubs: There are a number of national and area clubs catering for Lops. Contact addresses can be obtained from the BRC yearbook, or contact the BRC Secretary (address above).